Airedale Terriers

The Kendal and District Otterhound pack in the 1970s.

AIREDALE TERRIERS

AN OWNER'S COMPANION

**Mary Swash
and Donald Millar**

The Crowood Press

First published in 1991 by
The Crowood Press Ltd
Ramsbury, Marlborough
Wiltshire SN8 2HR

This impression 1994

British Library Cataloguing-in-Publication Data

Swash, Mary
  Airedale terriers.
  1. Terriers
  I. Title
  636.755

ISBN 1 85223 315 X

Picture credits

Frontispiece reproduced courtesy of Anne Roslin-Williams,
the photograph on page 65 by courtesy of Edwin Jacobs
and the photograph on page 88 by courtesy of Thomas Jeppsson.

Acknowledgements

Many thanks to Dawn Pearson for typing the manuscript, and to
Richard Packer MRCVS for help in preparing chapter 11.

Typeset by Context, Greenlea House, Green Street, Coopers Hill, Glos GL3 4RT
Printed and bound in Great Britain by BPCC Hazell Books Ltd

Contents

1

The History and Development of the Airedale Terrier

In the late eighteenth and early nineteenth centuries the Industrial Revolution transformed the face of Britain and nowhere more so than in the West Riding of Yorkshire. In a short space of time many new inventions changed the manufacture of woollen cloth from a cottage to a mill industry. The new machinery was driven by water power and the mills were located on the banks of the rivers which rose on the Pennine hills. Two of these rivers were the Aire and the Wharfe and it is here that our story begins.

Between 1760 and 1820 a new wave of Enclosure Acts either reduced the yeomanry to agricultural labourers or drove them off the land. This provided a ready source of labour for the mills and mines of the new towns. The miners and other working men in that part of the county of Yorkshire were well known as great sporting and betting men and their dogs played no small part in their leisure activities. Their dogs were often the small broken-haired terriers, black and tan dogs weighing some twenty pounds; although they were wonderful ratters and game and plucky scrappers, their lack of weight was against them when put in to fight trained Bull Terriers. It has been suggested that crosses with Bull Terriers were made to try to increase their weight and strength. There seems to be no real agreement as to what ingredients went into the Airedale mix but it is certain that the Otterhound played a part as, probably, did the Bull Terrier; both of these dogs were bigger and heavier than the broken-haired terrier and the addition of weight was necessary if the new dog was to fulfil its role.

Otter hunting was a popular local pastime and the Otterhound packs often had one or two terriers to flush out the quarry for the hounds. It is not impossible that the first mating between Terrier and Otterhound was an accidental liaison. The results, however, were so

7

favourable that more controlled crosses were carried out when the shrewd Yorkshire dogmen saw how successfully the new dog performed. Dog fighting was outlawed in Britain in 1835 (at the same time as the banning of bull-baiting and bear-baiting) but brutal fighting between trained dogs was still carried out secretly behind closed doors with large sums of money being bet on the results of the contest. The dogs generally used in the fights were Bull Terriers but on occasion this new terrier was put into the ring to fight the trained Bull Terrier. The old black and tan terrier would have been too light and not strong enough for dog fighting and so it was necessary to increase its weight and also to improve its fighting qualities. There are recorded instances of Airedales winning fights against trained fighting dogs. The fact that the Airedale had been classed as a terrier aroused some criticism because the dog was too big to go to earth as a terrier should; the Airedale however is defined as a terrier because of its origins, character and temperament.

J.H. Walsh was a man most critical of the courage shown by Airedale Terriers. He had at one time edited *The Field* and wrote under the pseudonym 'Stonehenge'. He is quoted as stating of the Airedale: 'He is considered by his opponents to lack heart in proportion to his size'. Walsh appeared to have received his information at second-hand from someone unnamed who claimed to have owned fourteen Airedales, none of them coming up to his idea of gameness. This correspondent based his verdict on the fact that none of his dogs would fight badgers or seemed to like scrapping with other dogs. Much of this is conjecture and can be called into question by remembering Colonel Richardson's preference for the Airedale Terrier as a war-dog and the choice of Airedale Terriers for police work by many forces world-wide. The reason offered later for the greater use of German Shepherd dogs was that they were more amenable to discipline whereas the Airedale showed an essential individuality that made him harder to mould. The increased use of the new terrier as a guard also helped to refute charges of cowardice. We all are aware that two dogs from the same litter can differ greatly in their behaviour in any given situation. One will stand his ground, while little relish for a fight will be shown by a litter-brother. In our experience the Airedale Terrier is not overtly aggressive, but does not turn the other cheek too readily and will defend quite robustly what he considers to be his.

The terrier that hunted rats along the riverbanks was still called the Waterside Terrier and there were classes for Waterside Terriers at the Otley and Bingley Agricultural Shows. A prominent dog lover, Hugh

Dalziel, did not particularly like this name, thinking it too general and not typifying the area where the dog had its roots. Writing in the County newspaper he suggested that it be changed and the dog called the Bingley Terrier. One reason was the support shown to the new breed at the Bingley Agricultural Shows and the large entries there in the classes for Waterside Terriers. There was a good deal of opposition to Dalziel's choice and the name Airedale Terrier was suggested as an alternative. The term Airedale Terrier stuck and so we have the name that has lasted for a hundred years – we cannot see its being changed now. Thus the Airedale Terrier began as a breed; there was mention in the records of the National Dog Show at Birmingham in 1883 and the 1886 Kennel Club Stud Book that for the first time had a separate section for Airedale Terriers. Today there are Airedales to be found wherever real dog lovers gather and anyone lucky enough to own an Airedale has a very special kind of dog.

Liverpool Police Dog Inspection 1919. The first police dog here was a pet Airedale Terrier taken on duty by his policeman owner – so successful was he that in April 1911 the committee purchased from Major Richardson six Airedale Terriers that had been specially trained for police work. The report states that 'they do regular tours of night duty and have proved to be of sound practical value'. They were placed for duty in the suburban areas of Fazakerley, West Derby, Old Swan, Wavertree, Aigburth Vale and Garston. Apparently the police today explain the absence of Airedale Terriers in the force as being due to the fact that they are offered only German Shepherds. Picture and information supplied by Mrs Maureen Allister.

The Airedale Terrier of the late nineteenth century was a very different dog from the Airedale of today. Firstly and probably most importantly he was a working dog; he was a show dog rather as an afterthought. Primarily the Airedale was a companion to his owner, essential to his leisure pastimes of ratting on the riverbanks, chasing otter, dog fighting and matches in the ratpits. It is rather doubtful if many of our modern show dogs would have the physique or stamina necessary to cope with the hard life of the early Airedale Terriers. Contemporary pictures show him to be longer in the back, far less elegant and altogether a much tougher character with fewer furnishings than seem essential today. As well as hunting rats and other river animals, the Airedale was in a large way responsible for the eradication of two pests that were then quite common in the Yorkshire Dales. The pine marten and the pole cat were vermin, and very destructive of poultry and game, but by the turn of the century they seemed to have disappeared from the north of England. By this time the Airedale Terrier had emerged as a definite type.

Early Airedales

Kennel Club rules in 1886 stated that in order to become a champion a dog must have won seven first prizes, three of which must have been in Challenge classes and one of these three at a Kennel Club show or at the National Dog Show Society in Birmingham. The remaining four wins had to be at Open shows. A change to the rules in 1890 brought a 'points' system into operation with a number of two-point shows announced each year; otherwise every Kennel Club show win counted as one point. Ten points were required to make up a champion. By 1892 a new system, not unlike the one in use today, was in operation. There must have been a good deal of controversy for the changes to have been made so rapidly. However, this new system settled down and was used for some years; only some small changes were necessary to create the system that we use today. A dog called Newbold Test was the first ever Airedale Champion in the year 1891. Newbold Test was bred by Mr Deanley, his sire was Guess and his dam was Jenny. Champions also made up in 1891 were Rustic Lad, by Charley out of Nell, and Wharfdale Rush whose pedigree is not recorded. A Mr W. Tatham owned both Newbold Test and Wharfdale Rush. The first bitch Champion, also made up in 1891 was Vixen III bred and owned by A. Walker. The sire was Rover III and the dam Young Floss.

Ch. Wharfedale Rush – one of the first ever champions but he had no recorded pedigree!

A number of kennels with registered affixes came into being all over Britain although there was not the tight control that we have today and names of dogs and affixes were changed quite frequently. Although at that time pedigrees were not very reliable, a few names of recognized sires have been preserved. Rover III was born in 1881 and sired two good bitches: Ch. Vixen III and Ch. Venus III; Wharfdale Rover was another of his offspring who did well in the show ring. An Airedale Terrier that never became a champion, but nevertheless made a marked impression on the breed was Airedale Jerry. Airedale Jerry's colouring was excellent and though not particularly good in head he had a strong and well-proportioned body and he always seemed to pass on these two qualities to his offspring. Many of the best bloodlines originate from Airedale Jerry through his son Ch. Cholmondeley Briar, whose dam was Cholmondeley Luce. Sired by Cholmondeley Briar were Willow Nut and Briar Test and in turn Briar Test was the father of Master Briar, said to be one of the pillars of the breed.

Some of the most famous Airedales of all time were the offspring of Master Briar, names that read like a catalogue of Terrier greats: the

11

Ch. Cholmondeley Briar – Airedale Jerry's most famous son and in the opinion of Holland Buckley 'one of the soundest dogs in my memory'.

world-famous Ch. Clonmel Monarch as well as Towyn Masterpiece, Crompton Marvel, Mistress Royal and Rock King. It was permissible to buy in a dog and then change the name and affix to suit the new owner. Holland Buckley in his book *The Airedale Terrier* tells of the mating of Clipper to Cholmondeley Mona with a resulting litter of nine, one of which, Warfield Victor, was entered in a £3 selling class at a small show in Reading. The dog won second prize and the owner of the winner, a Bedlington, enforced the claiming clause much to the chagrin of Victor's owner. Within twenty-four hours, Royston Mills and Holland Buckley had become the new owners of Victor and he was subsequently renamed Clonmel Marvel. To quote Holland Buckley again: 'Marvel downed every dog or bitch in the strongest competition, frequently being the recipient of cups for the best dog in the show'. Ch. Clonmel Marvel put up a record eighteen successive Championships. Later he was exported to the United States.

The Clonmel affix first appears in 1895 and was owned by Mrs Mills, then Royston Mills went into partnership with Holland Buckley and

*Ch. Clonmel Monarch – a great winner in England and in America
– the owners were highly criticized for selling this dog 'that could
have set the type for all time'. Before leaving these shores Monarch
sired some outstanding stock – ten champions are credited to him –
whether they are all English champions is not clear.*

they shared the Clonmel affix. Ch. Clonmel Marvel was the first
champion made up by this kennel; later in 1900 Clonmel Kitty was
also made a champion and in 1901 Clonmel Monarch was made up.
There was certainly some latitude and flexibility in the attitude as
owners bought dogs and applied their own affixes and changed
names. There were other owners who were very successful at the
turn of the century and afterwards: G.H. Elder of Taunton with the
Tone Kennel and Mr A. Jennings with Dumbarton Lass (he also later
owned Master Briar). On the break up of the Dumbarton Kennel,
many of the dogs including Master Briar and Dumbarton Lass came
into the possession of Mr Stuart Noble, although a Mr T. Kershaw
later appears to have been the owner of Ch. Dumbarton Sceptre, Ch.
Dumbarton Rattler and Ch. Dumbarton Sunflower. The Clonmel
Kennel continued to make up Champion Airedales until just before the

*Ch. Dumbarton Lass – bought at a show for £25.00, 'Lass' beat
nearly all comers for two or three seasons shows – she ended up in
Montreal.*

First World War which interrupted the dog show scene from 1917 to
1920. Captain Banes Condy claimed that breeders had mistakenly bred
Airedales too large ending up with a sixty-pound dog and the result
was disastrous. A new group of Airedale fanciers appeared just before
the war and these men formed the nucleus of the post-war kennels.

Hildebrand Wilson was a very proficient dog handler, and able to
trim a dog very expertly. He made up his first Champion, Wrose
Blossom in 1912, but his best-known dog was Ch. Wrose Monarch,
litter brother to Ch. Clonmel Cuddle-Up and Ch. Brincham Beta. These
champions were all sired by Ch. Warland Ditto from J.P. Hall's
Warland Kennel in north-east England. This kennel had a profound
effect on the subsequent quality of the breed and the Warland strain
can be found in the extended pedigrees of many of the best modern
Airedale Terriers. Ch. Warland Whatnot, Ch. Warland Ditto, Ch. Warland Strategy, and Ch. Warland Waterman are some of the very
successful dogs from this famous kennel. Jimmy Gray, our most senior
Airedaler began his dog career as a kennel boy at Warland. Old

Ch. Tone Masterpiece – one of several famous dogs from this West Country Kennel – his career here seems to have been 'up and down' but in America he was seldom beaten.

pedigrees show how closely the Warland and Wrose kennels worked together with dogs from one being mated to bitches from the other.

Training for War

There was another very substantial figure in the Airedale world in the early days of this century: Major (later Colonel) Richardson was a great dog lover, and also a brilliant dog trainer. He trained many breeds but his affections lay mainly with Airedales which he considered the most versatile of all dogs. Although in Colonel Richardson, Britain had one of the greatest dog trainers, we as a nation had no official training programme for war-dogs. Many senior army officers believed that there was a definite need for war-dogs to act either as sentries, or as messengers, or as ambulance dogs to locate wounded soldiers. Both France and Germany had war-dog training establishments both of which Richardson visited as an observer. He was very impressed by what he saw and managed to convince many individual senior army officers of the suitability of certain breeds of dog. Although not yet official policy, a number of Regiments of the British Army purchased dogs trained by Colonel Richardson.

Early in the First World War the War Office decided that because of an ever-increasing number of requests for messenger dogs, the building of a training establishment at Shoeburyness should be started. Major Richardson was invited to take charge of the Official Dog Training School. Richardson closed his house and moved his kennels and his dogs to the new war-dog school. From here many dogs were sent to the war front. The heavy demand for messenger dogs caused such pressure at Shoeburyness that it was decided to move the school to Lyndhurst in the New Forest. A special railway train carried the 100 men and 250 dogs and their luggage and equipment, completing the move very rapidly. Altogether, 7,000 dogs died on active service during the First World War and some of the deeds performed by the war-dogs showed remarkable understanding and intelligence. Stories abound which illustrate the courage and fortitude of these dogs and many a Tommy owed his life to their bravery. Between the Wars the Richardsons continued to train dogs, mainly as guards, and Airedale Terriers were his chosen favourite breed. Many police forces used Airedales as night patrol dogs. When the Second World War broke out, Colonel Richardson laid plans before the War Office but because of increasing age, he handed over the running and training to younger men. Dogs were used as sentries and for red-cross duties but few dogs saw active service.

This verse was written after the First World War by William Wilson, a well-known Lancashire Airedaler whose Mitterdale affix still appears in some of the older pedigrees. The verse illustrates those qualities possessed by the Airedale Terrier and valued by the armed forces and police forces in the 1920s–1940s.

DOGS OF WAR
The Airedale

A call came from over the sea,
For a dog to do duty for his own country.
The demand for a breed that would never fail,
The choice without doubt was our hardy Airedale.

His job to carry messages to and fro;
Often he passed in sight of the foe.
Through mud and shell fire, across rivers and floods,
He would carry on bravely whatever the odds.

Many were the hardships he had to endure,
But he never failed, of this we are sure.

From dug-out, over trench, he quickly sped,
Across no man's land, strewn with the dead.

When at last to headquarters he came through the fight,
He was welcomed with food and bed for the night.
All ready for the fray the following day,
As full of life as a boy full of play.

What more can we say of our gallant breed,
He answered the call of his country's need.
He did all that was asked and did it well,
Then returned home victorious, our brave Airedale.

The Airedale was trained by a man of fame,
Lieutenant Colonel Richardson was his name.
He knew the dangers and hardships too,
But he knew our breed would pull us through.

The gradually changing face of society has altered the role played in Britain by the Airedale Terrier. Increasing urbanization and a more sophisticated population has made a difference in the leisure activities of the working men who generally owned Airedales. The Airedale is no longer worked in this country – otter hunting and badger baiting are illegal and ratting competitions are a thing of the past. Few of the dogs' specialized skills are required any longer and may be in danger of dying out. The Airedale is a dog with great stamina. Some years ago we had one of our dogs out on the Lakeland Fells – we were there all day in torrential rain – but only after hours of appalling weather did the dog's waterproof jacket let her down. Back in the dry and wrapped in a warm blanket after a brisk rub down, she was her normal self again. She lived to the age of fifteen and was making the lives of local foxes a misery until the day she died.

Many of the Airedales' inherent qualities remain dormant waiting to be released. A fairly recent leisure activity seems to have been specially tailored for the Airedale and to see an Airedale happily sprinting round the agility ring is quite a joy. The dog quite obviously enjoys the challenge and the only requisite for entry is physical fitness for handler as well as for dog, and any breed can try the obstacles. The intent but happy face of the agility dog is often preferable to the wooden look of the show dog. If we are not careful, concentrating only on the showing side, we could destroy the qualities that really make the dog tick and then we shall have lost the true Airedale spirit.

2

Pedigrees

Most Airedale Terrier owners will be quite familiar with the appearance of a pedigree – the diagrammatic record of a dog's ancestry. A pedigree is or should be given with other documents to every buyer of a pure-bred puppy. The word pedigree stems from the Middle French phrase *Pie' de Grue* meaning Crane's Foot. The lines of the crane's foot represent the parental lines of the animal. From the pedigree, it is possible to trace the ancestry of any pure-bred dog or, of course, any other pure-bred animal. Pedigrees can go back for many

Pedigree of Ch. Master Briar – line bred to Airedale Jerry the dog who is usually given credit for founding such a wonderful line of winners.

Ch. Master Briar – said by many to be the pillar of the breed and noted for his head, judged to be the best seen up to that time.

many generations and are similar to family trees. For example, the Supreme Champion at Crufts in 1986, Ch. Ginger Xmas Carol can be traced through a six-generation pedigree back to Ch. Riverina Tweedsbairn, the 1961 Crufts Top Dog.

The most usual form of pedigree is a simple geometrical progression, the number of names doubling with each generation. The natural artistic talents of man have meant that there have been many ingenious embellishments to try to give pedigrees a more attractive look. A most distinctive example is the circular pedigree in which the dog in question is in the centre and each preceding generation occupies a further concentric ring. In a pedigree, dogs that have achieved the status of Champion are usually written in red. A ten-generation pedigree will contain the names of two thousand and forty-five dogs; the preparation and checking of this is no mean feat.

In 1874 the first Kennel Club Stud Book was published. It was compiled by Frank Pearce, printed by *The Field* for the Kennel Club and covers the period 1859 to 1874. Among other information such as show results, rules and regulations it gives as many one-generation pedigrees as were then available. The breeds numbered forty and

Ch. Jokyl Gallipants – the Top Dog All Breeds in 1983, twice Best of Breed at Crufts and currently the Top Sire in the breed with eleven English champions to his credit. His sire Ch. Siccawei Galliard is the Top Sire of the breed and his dam Ch. Jokyl Smartie Pants the Top Brood Bitch.

naturally Airedale Terriers were not among that number since the breed was not recognized by the Kennel Club until July 1884; they appeared in the Kennel Club Stud Book of 1886. The first mention in the pedigree section of this Stud Book is J.M. Edwards' 'Bobbas' (18314), born about 1882. In the pedigree section of the 1885 Stud Book under Broken-haired Terriers is a bitch called Airedale Lass – this is the first mention of an Airedale in the pedigree section. The first actual mention of an Airedale Terrier is to be found in the Stud Book for 1884 in the Dog Show results for the British Kennel Association Dog Show at Aston in May 1883 where the winner is given as T. Carr's Keighley Crack, 2nd was A. Walker's Rover III and 3rd H.C. Grove's Roy. All

Ch. Siccawei Galliard	Ch. Bengal Flamboyant	Bengal Buldeo	Ch. Bengal Mowgli	Ch. Bengal Gunga Din / Bengal Thunderbird
			Ch. Bengal Suliston Merry Maid	Ch. Bengal Gunga Din / Suliston Psyche
		Ch. Bengal Springtime	Ch. Bengal Brulyn Sahib	Ch. Bengal Gunga Din / Brulyn Brimful
			Ch. Bengal Begum	Bengal Leander / Ch. Bengal Kresent Ballerina
	Ch. Siccawei Impudent Miss	Ch. Bengal Fastnet	Ch. Bengal Kresent Brave	Bengal Bladud / Kresent Model Maid
			Bengal Chippinghey Fircone	Ch. Mayjack Briar / Chippinghey Deep Loam
		Ch. Siccawei Princess Pam	Ch. Riverina Tweedsbairn	Ch. Riverina Tweed / Ch. Riverina Diana of Siccawei
			Ch. Siccawei Artemis	Siccawei Marquis / Ch. Riverina Diana of Siccawei
Ch. Jokyl Smartie Pants	Ch. Jokyl Smart Guy	Ch. Bengal Flamboyant	Bengal Buldeo	Ch. Bengal Mowgli / Ch. Bengal Suliston Merry Maid
			Ch. Bengal Springtime	Ch. Bengal Brulyn Sahib / Ch. Bengal Begum
		Ch. Jokyl Elegance	Ch. Jokyl Bengal Figaro	Ch. Bengal Kresent Brave / Bengal Chippinghey Fircone
			Jokyl Hera	Ch. Jokyl Othello v Kirm / Ch. Jokyl Top of the Form
	Jokyl Dollyrocker	Ch. Jokyl Space Leader	Ch. Jokyl Bengal Figaro	Ch. Bengal Kresent Brave / Bengal Chippinghey Fircone
			Ch. Jokyl Top of the Form	Turkish Rural Cavalier / Chippinghey Deep Loam
		Kenlucky Katrina	Jokyl Chippinghey Kestrel	Ch. Jokyl Space Leander / Ch. Jokyl Chippinghey Greensleeves
			Kenlucky Desdemona	Ch. Jokyl Othello v Kirm / Kenlucky LooLoo

GALLIPANTS' PEDIGREE – Date of Birth 23 August 1981

three of these dogs are listed in the pedigree section as Broken-haired Scotch or Yorkshire Terriers.

In the first Stud Book in a section on pedigrees, non-sporting, is a list under Black and Tan Terriers (except Toys) – these are possibly the forerunners of our present-day Airedale Terriers, but Rover III appears in the 1886 Stud Book as an Airedale Terrier with the Stud Book number (13825). In earlier Stud Books Rover III is shown with the same number as a Broken-haired Terrier. Making use of the information contained in the Kennel Club Stud Books, it is possible to trace the ancestry of a particular dog. The achievement of a certain standard gives the dog an entry in the Stud Book. With the entry the dog receives a Stud Book number. The two letters at the end of the number indicate in which Stud Book the names of sire and dam are to be found. This process can be continued for each of the parents, then the grandparents, thus gradually building up the pedigree.

Line Breeding

Many breeders carry out a programme called line breeding where a close study of pedigrees is used in order to breed in certain qualities. Others make use of their knowledge of the various characteristics of dogs to utilize pedigrees in the choice of sire or dam. The danger of line breeding is the presence of both dominant and recessive genes in the chromosones. The desired characteristic may be carried by a recessive gene while the dominant gene could produce something quite disastrous. A pedigree may be useful to help in the selection of sire and dam for mating if certain general principles are observed. All that can be learned from a pedigree are the names of an animal's forebears. One wishes of course that the latest name on the pedigree will live up to the qualities of his parents and grandparents. It may be found, however, that most severe hereditary defects have been passed to many animals quite unknowingly. The geneticist finds many other pieces of information from a pedigree. Degrees of inbreeding are seen, hereditary defects can be traced and the animals carrying the defects can be identified. Breeders do use pedigrees to gather information in order to practise line breeding or the mating of near relatives. Inbreeding is the mating of parents to children or brother with sister.

Mass selection is where the breeder chooses from those which are nearest to his ideal type using pedigrees and his knowledge of conformation. More effective breeding comes from progeny testing. In

Ch. Riverina Tweedsbairn – the top winning Airedale of all time, with the title of Top Dog All Breeds in 1960 and 1961 and winner of Best in Show at Crufts 1961. The Top Dog All Breeds 1983 Gallipants and the 1986 Crufts Best in Show winner Ch. Ginger Xmas Carol are descended from him through the great sire Ch. Siccawei Galliard.

the dog shows of some countries, there are Progeny classes and these classes can give an indication of what type of dog can be expected from particular matings or from a particular sire or dam.

It can be a real joy to see a proud parent leading in his or her progeny, if they are all of a type and in good trim; nothing is more impressive than the sight of their parading. The study of pedigrees is a fascinating hobby as is trying to find photographs of all the dogs in a pedigree to see how the latest shape up and who they resemble.

We hope that in this book there will be one or two photographs of the dogs in your Airedale's pedigree. A look at both the pedigrees will reveal that in 1897 breeders were line breeding, as they were in 1981.

The British Breed Standard

(Reproduced by kind permission of the Kennel Club of Great Britain)

General Appearance

Largest of the terriers, a muscular, active, fairly cobby dog, without suspicion of legginess or undue length of body.

Characteristics

Keen of expression, quick of movement, on the tip-toe of expectation at any movement. Character denoted and shown by expression of eyes, and by carriage of ears and erect tail.

Temperament

Outgoing and confident, friendly, courageous and intelligent. Alert at all times; not aggressive but fearless.

Head and Skull

Skull long and flat, not too broad between ears, and narrowing slightly to eyes. Well balanced, with no apparent difference in length between skull and foreface. Free from wrinkles, with stop hardly visible; cheeks level and free from fullness. Foreface well-filled up before eyes, not dishfaced or falling away quickly below eyes, but a delicate chiselling prevents appearance of wedginess or plainness. Upper and lower jaws deep, powerful, strong and muscular, as strength of foreface is greatly desired. No excess development of the jaws to give a rounded or bulging appearance to the cheeks, as 'cheekiness' is undesirable. Lips tight, nose black.

Eyes

Dark in colour, small, not prominent, full of terrier expression, keenness and intelligence. Light or bold eye highly undesirable.

Ears

'V' shaped with a side carriage; small but not out of proportion to size of dog. Topline of folded ear slightly above level of skull. Pendulous ears or ears set too high undesirable.

Mouth

Teeth strong. Jaws strong. Scissor bite, i.e. upper teeth closely overlapping the lower teeth and set square to the jaws preferable, but vice-like bite acceptable. An overshot or undershot mouth undesirable.

24

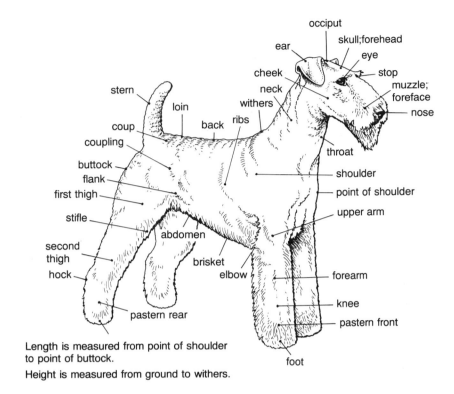

Points of the Airedale Terrier.

The labels in the diagram:

occiput
skull;forehead
ear
eye
cheek
stop
neck
muzzle; foreface
stern
withers
nose
loin
back
ribs
coup
coupling
throat
buttock
shoulder
flank
point of shoulder
first thigh
upper arm
stifle
second thigh
abdomen
hock
forearm
brisket
elbow
knee
pastern rear
pastern front
foot

Length is measured from point of shoulder to point of buttock.

Height is measured from ground to withers.

Neck

Clean, muscular, of moderate length and thickness, gradually widening towards shoulders, and free from throatiness.

Forequarters

Shoulders long, well laid back, sloping obliquely; shoulder blades flat. Forelegs perfectly straight with good bone. Elbows perpendicular to body, working free of sides.

Body

Back short, strong, straight and level, showing no slackness. Loins muscular. Ribs well sprung. In short-coupled and well ribbed-up dogs

25

there is little space between ribs and hips. When dog is long in couplings some slackness will be shown here. Chest deep (i.e. approximately level with elbows), but not broad.

Hindquarters

Thighs long and powerful with muscular second thigh, stifles well bent, turned neither in nor out. Hocks well let down, parallel with each other when viewed from behind.

Feet

Small, round and compact, with a good depth of pad, well cushioned, and toes moderately arched, turning neither in nor out.

Tail

Set on high and carried gaily, not curled over back. Good strength and substance. Customarily docked. Tip approximately at same height as top of skull.

Gait/Movement

Legs carried straight forward. Forelegs move freely parallel to the sides. When approaching forelegs should form a continuation of the straight line of the front, feet being same distance apart as elbows. Propulsive power is furnished by hind legs.

Coat

Hard, dense and wiry, not so long as to appear ragged. Lying straight and close, covering body and legs; outer coat hard wiry and stiff, undercoat shorter and softer. Hardest coats are crinkling or just slightly waved; curly or soft coat highly undesirable.

Colour

Body saddle black or grizzle as top of the neck and top surface of tail. All other parts tan. Ears often a darker tan, and shading may occur round neck and side of skull. A few white hairs, between forelegs acceptable.

Size

Height about 58–61cms (23–24ins) for dogs, taken from top of shoulder, and bitches about 56–59cms (22–23ins).

Faults

Any departure from the foregoing points should be considered a fault and the seriousness with which the fault should be regarded should be in exact proportion to its degree.

Note

Male animals should have two apparently normal testicles fully descended into the scrotum.

The American Breed Standard

(Reproduced by kind permission of the American Kennel Club)

Head

Should be well balanced with little apparent difference between the length of skull and foreface.

Skull

Should be long and flat, not too broad between the ears and narrowing very slightly to the eyes. Scalp should be free from wrinkles, stop hardly visible and cheeks level and free from fullness.

Ears

Should be V-shaped with carriage rather to the side of the head, not pointing to the eyes, small but not out of proportion to the size of the dog. The topline of the folded ear should be above the level of the skull.

Foreface

Should be deep, powerful, strong and muscular. Should be well-filled up before the eyes.

Eyes

Should be dark, small, not prominent, full of terrier expression, keenness and intelligence.

Lips

Should be black and not too small.

Teeth

Should be strong and white, free from discoloration or defect. Bite either level or vise-like. A slightly over-lapping or scissor bite is permissible without preference.

Neck

Should be of moderate length and thickness gradually widening towards the shoulders. Skin tight, not loose.

Shoulders and Chest

Shoulders long and sloping well into the back. Shoulder blades flat. From the front, chest deep but not broad. The depth of the chest should be approximately on a level with the elbows.

Body

Back should be short, strong and level. Ribs well sprung. Loins muscular and of good width. There should be but little space between the last rib and the hip joint.

Hindquarters

Should be strong and muscular with no droop.

Tail

The root of the tail should be set well up on the back. It should be carried gaily but not curled over the back. It should be of good strength and substance and of fair length.

Legs

Forelegs should be perfectly straight, with plenty of muscle and bone.

Elbows

Should be perpendicular to the body, working free of sides.

Thighs

Should be long and powerful with muscular second thigh, stifles well bent, not turned either in or out, hocks well let down and parallel with each other when viewed from behind.

Feet

Should be small, round and compact with a good depth of pad, well cushioned; the toes moderately arched, not turned either in or out.

Coat

Should be hard, dense and wiry, lying straight and close, covering the dog well over the body and legs. Some of the hardest are crinkling or just slightly waved. At the base of the hard, very stiff hair should be a shorter growth of softer hair termed the undercoat.

Color

The head and ears should be tan, the ears being of a darker shade than the rest. Dark markings on either side of the skull are permissible. The legs up to the thighs and elbows and the underpart of the body and chest are also tan and the tan frequently runs into the shoulder. The sides and upper parts of the body should be black or dark grizzle. A red mixture is often found in the black and is not to be considered objectionable. A small white blaze on the chest is characteristic of certain strains of the breed.

Size

Dogs should measure approximately 23 inches in height at the shoulder; bitches, slightly less. Both sexes should be sturdy, well muscled and boned.

Movement

Movement or action is the crucial test of conformation. Movement should be free. As seen from the front the forelegs should swing perpendicular from the body free from the sides, the feet the same distance apart as the elbows. As seen from the rear the hind legs should be parallel with each other, neither too close nor too far apart, but so placed as to give a strong, well-balanced stance and movement. The toes should not be turned either in or out.

Faults

Yellow eyes, hound ears, white feet, soft coat, being much over or under the size limit, being undershot or overshot, having poor movement, are faults that should be severely penalized.

SCALE OF POINTS

Head	10	Coat	10
Neck, shoulders and chest	10	Color	5
Body	10	Size	10
Hindquarters and tail	10	Movement	10
Legs and feet	10	General characteristics and expression	15
		TOTAL	100

30

3

Buying a Puppy

The Airedale Terrier is a very intelligent and strong dog, playful and with a great sense of fun. He is very loyal and his strong instinct is to guard his family and property – in short we think that there is nothing quite like an Airedale. Colonel Richardson, after a study of various breeds, chose the Airedale Terrier as the most suitable breed to train as companions and as guard-dogs before the First World War. This meant that the Airedale became more widely known – it is not so many years since people spoke of 'Colonel Richardson Airedales' as though they were a breed apart. Colonel Richardson trained Airedales to track by scent, guard and carry messages in the war, proving that the breed can be taught to do anything if the training method is the right one. Airedales were used also as police dogs and in fact are employed for that purpose in Japan today. Any of these are good reasons for choosing an Airedale!

Now we are faced with the question of whether to choose a young puppy or an older dog, a dog or a bitch. Buying a very young puppy of about eight weeks of age is a good idea if there are young children in the house as obviously they can be brought up together. The child must learn to respect the puppy, not to tease it and to help to attend to its needs, and at the same time the puppy must learn to be gentle with the child. In most cases puppies become wild only if they are encouraged to do so. Remember, it may be quite amusing for the puppy to leap about and be naughty when it is still small, but this small puppy will grow into a very large Airedale, weighing about sixty pounds and standing twenty-two to twenty-four inches high at the shoulder. When a dog of that size behaves badly he will be no joy to himself or anyone else. It is important to start training the puppy with firmness but kindness right from the start. When choosing your puppy take him away from the others to see how he behaves and responds to you. It may be interesting to find out if the puppy has been aptitude tested, to see if he has the essential qualities that you are looking for in your companion. You should remember that, with luck,

Typical inquisitive Airedale Terrier puppies.

you are going to live with this new friend for a decade or more. Although the way that you have trained him will to a great extent govern the way that he will behave, his character should really be compatible with yours.

If you decide that you want to start with an older dog, find out all you can about the way he has been brought up and how he has spent his days: has he been socialized at all? If he has spent many months in kennels and has never been in a house, you are going to need a lot of patience and time teaching him all the things that we accept as normal. Machines such as hoovers or mixers are very frightening for a dog that has never heard them before. If the dog seems nervous at first give him time to get used to it all before writing him off as a neurotic. Any reputable breeder should take a dog back if he does not settle down after a reasonable trial period, but there are very few Airedales that do not appreciate being the one and only beloved pet instead of one of a crowd, however good the conditions at the kennel where he was born and raised.

If you want to take on another sort of older dog there are always the unfortunates that have fallen on hard times – the so called rescue dogs. Most of these come up for rehoming through no fault of their own but because of bereavement, divorce, the former owner going abroad or a wife who did not go out to work but now has to. Usually they are really super animals – some well trained – others not, and here again a careful study of the background, if it is known, is essential, and also a good length of time allocated to getting him used to the routines of his new home.

Choosing a Puppy for Showing

If your interests lie in the direction of dog shows, there are other points to consider besides the character of the puppy, although obviously this is also of paramount importance. Once you have decided on the type of Airedale that you admire and have chosen a breeder, approach him to see if he has any puppies to sell and ask his advice. Study the pedigrees and be prepared to wait for the right dog to become available – make sure that the puppy is registered and the transfer is signed. If you are purchasing a fairly young puppy there is absolutely no guarantee that it will turn out into a super show dog – there is so much that may go wrong – the second teeth may not come in properly or the puppy may grow too much, or not enough, or a very promising puppy may turn into a really plain adult. This is a chance that we all

A very important passenger.

take when running on puppies that we have bred and this is what makes the whole thing so fascinating and exciting. If an animal that one has run on does turn out to be all one had hoped, that is the ultimate reward for all the hard work and dedication.

If you want to start showing right away it is advisable to buy the best show dog or bitch that you can afford. Personally we would not recommend the purchase of a male dog if you want to start breeding show stock – after all, if you have a bitch she can always be mated to the best dog in the country. Before making a decision go to as many shows as you can and watch the Airedales being judged to see if there are any that you like the look of. If there are, approach the owners to see if any of them are for sale. If you are buying a bitch as a foundation to a kennel that you hope will produce winners, study the pedigrees well and ascertain if the bloodlines are winner-producing or if this is a one off (that is, the only good one to come from a mediocre lot). Try to buy a bitch with as few faults as possible and one that is a typical Airedale, sound of structure and with a good character and also with true Airedale expression – namely good ears and eyes (bad ear carriage and large, bold or light eyes are very hard faults to breed out) and of course a good mouth with a full set of teeth. If the bitch in question is being shown, her temperament can be observed.

Although it will obviously cost a lot more for an older animal you can see exactly what you are getting for your money. If you are going to buy a young puppy hoping that it will be a show prospect, place yourself in the hands of the breeder that you have decided to purchase from; use his experience and honesty, and also the knowledge that you have picked up by studying the dogs and the pedigrees and 'go over' the puppy or puppies that he may have to offer you.

'Go over' means placing the puppy on the table and assessing its virtues and faults (of course it will have some faults). See if the head is typical – almost flat from nose to occiput with clean flat cheeks and well built-up under the eyes – in fact shaped like a brick. The eyes should be well shaped, slightly oval, deep set and showing a little wickedness and fun, small and with no redness in the corners. Colour is hard to determine at eight weeks as they may still have a bluish haze and the true colour cannot be seen until three to four months of age. The neck should be long and flow into the back, the topline should be level and the body well ribbed with a deep chest – the front legs should be straight and the hindquarters sturdy with a good bend of stifle. The coat should be of a good colour and the harder the better but some are quite fluffy as pups. By looking into the roots of the leg

front view

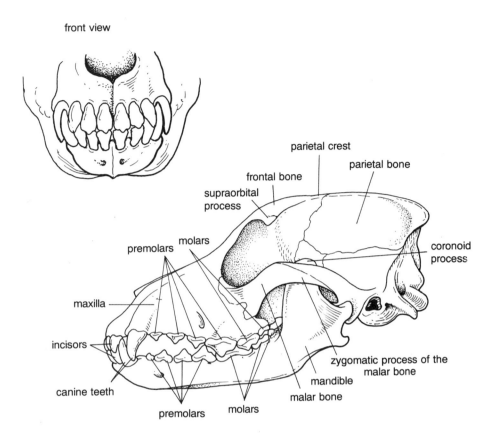

parietal crest

parietal bone

frontal bone

supraorbital
process

molars

premolars

maxilla

incisors

canine teeth

premolars

molars

coronoid
process

zygomatic process of the
malar bone

mandible

malar bone

The skull and dentition of the Airedale.

hair and coat one can see if the colour is deeper there and sometimes the coat texture is harder as well which is all to the good. The real fluffy or 'sheep coat' must be avoided at all costs and no worthy breeder would offer one as a show prospect.

Try to get the puppy to move up and down so that you can see if it is going straight and true. Even at an early age you can tell if it is cow-hocked, open-hocked (bow-legged), out at the elbows or if the feet are splayed. Most Airedale puppies look as if they have large feet but if they are fairly tight, high-arched and cat-like they are alright.

Examine the teeth and make sure that the bite is correct, that the top incisors overlap the lower ones, that the canines are correctly placed:

the lower canines should be outside the top canines and not growing into the upper palate. Even though the puppy may have a perfect mouth with the first or milk teeth, this can change with the second teeth and great attention should be paid to the mouth when the milk teeth are being shed and the new ones are coming through. It may be that one or more of the milk teeth need to be extracted if they are causing the permanent teeth to grow incorrectly.

Size in a young puppy is quite a difficult thing to determine, but usually the leggy, racy puppy will end up taller than the thicker, cobbier type. Face the fact that the puppy will go through some very ugly stages as some parts will grow while others do not and at times you will despair. Have faith: in time it will all come together if it was there to start with! Some puppies take a very long time, so patience is the name of the game.

General Points to Look For

Whether the puppy is to be a pet or a show hopeful, it should look really fit – its coat in good condition and eyes bright and full of fun. Typical Airedale puppies will charge around looking for something to play with and mischief to get into. Their actions at this age are really intriguing and one could happily spend hours just watching them – they are real time-wasters! This is actually a good way to decide on which puppy really stands out and shows the style and dominance that is so essential in a good show dog – that extra indefinable 'something special' that makes it hard to be overlooked in the show ring. The right mental attitude is so important: a puppy should come forward and be happy to see people, wagging its tail and looking a picture of health. Take plenty of time choosing your puppy – this is a big decision and not one to be taken lightly.

Earlier we mentioned aptitude testing and this is an excellent way to determine whether the puppy has the aptitude for the job that he is required to do. Although to a certain extent the early experiences and training will influence his behaviour, he has also inherited charac-teristics that will show themselves at a very early age. The tests should be carried out at seven weeks of age, each puppy on its own in a room or area new to it, before a meal and not on a day when they have been wormed, are unwell or have been inoculated. The test should be done by someone unknown to the puppies. Basically the idea is to team up the right dogs to the right owners and so with luck have fewer dogs

Dinner is served.

having to be 'rescued' because they are in the wrong situation. The tests can show if a particular puppy will have the right combination of traits to suit the new owner.

Early Days and Training

When the great decision has been made, ask the breeder for a diet sheet and make sure that it is quite clear what the puppy has been fed on – if the diet is to be changed, do it gradually after the puppy has had time to adjust to its new home. Ask the breeder to show you the correct way to groom the puppy and we advise that he is groomed every day so that he becomes used to the discipline imposed by doing this. Do not let the puppy get away with behaving badly when having his legs and beard brushed and combed or he will end up as the boss. Our puppies are groomed from about three weeks of age and, when they leave us, are quite used to it. It is quite alarming how many dogs that come back for trimming are very matted and really badly behaved while the litter mates that we have kept allow us to do anything without a grumble. Admittedly though, some are born fidgets and try the odd delaying tactic – a front paw waving pathetically, or sitting down, and one bitch always yawns in an exaggerated way as soon as her head and expression are trimmed. Apart from all these considerations, daily grooming keeps the coat in good condition by removing the dead hair, and also enables one to see at once if anything is wrong with the skin, ears or eyes.

If the breeder offers insurance, take it and if not make enquiries about taking out cover for the puppy as soon as it is taken from the breeder. Most veterinary surgeons have particulars of insurance companies and in any case it is a good idea to get a veterinary surgeon lined up to see to the inoculations for the puppy. These should be done as soon as possible after leaving the breeder. The inoculations are against hard pad, distemper, hepatitis, leptospirosis, parainfluenza and parvovirus, all of which can be killers. The course will usually consist of two or three injections, depending on the age of the puppy, and the veterinary surgeon will give a certificate which will have the details of all inoculations given. Keep this certificate as it will be needed if the puppy has to be put into a boarding kennel at any time. It will also have the date when the booster inoculations are due. No reputable boarding kennel will accept an animal that is not fully covered against these dreadful diseases. It is essential for the puppy's welfare and your peace of mind that these precautions are taken at the correct time.

Airedales have a great sense of fun.

Before taking the puppy or older dog home make sure that everything is ready – food, bowls, grooming equipment, collar and lead, bed, or kennel if it is to be a kennel dog. Make sure that the garden is well fenced-in and a secure gate fixed that can be opened and closed easily by humans but that the puppy, or adult Airedale as it will soon become, cannot. Airedale Terriers are very clever and soon learn to open doors and gates. We had a bitch at one time who used to open the run gate so that her pals could get out and run off while she stayed inside looking so smug as if to say 'Look how good I am not running away'! We have to put round door knobs on our doors as the Airedales push lever handles down and let themselves in or out at will. Even so, the really determined characters will find a way to manipulate round door knobs with their teeth, though so far they cannot actually unlock doors!

Puppies are inclined to exercise their teeth on anything that is handy, so it is best to use plastic beds and old blankets until this stage has passed.

4

Breeding

Most Airedale Terrier bitches come into season twice a year, the first time is often at seven or eight months but it may not occur until as late as fifteen or sixteen months. Some bitches only come into season once a year and this is nothing to worry about. Airedales are slow-maturing dogs so it is as well not to try to breed from them until they have had at least three seasons or are eighteen to twenty-four months old. The new Kennel Club code recommends that bitches do not have more than one litter a year and this is sound advice if the pups are to be born strong and healthy.

When deciding whether to mate your bitch or not, many factors must be taken into consideration. Firstly, if your bitch has been purchased purely as a pet, find out whether she has enough good attributes to pass on to her puppies, including a good temperament. Is she sound? Has she had her hips X-rayed and scored with a reasonable result? Does she have a good mouth and ears?

Another point to consider is whether you really need to breed a litter. Have you potential customers waiting for a puppy from your particular bitch, do you want to breed from her to have a puppy to keep for yourself, and have you the time and the facilities to be able to look after a possible fourteen or so puppies? Yes, we do mean that – seventeen puppies have been born to and reared by Airedale bitches. This means a lot of work, and cleaning up after them until they are eight weeks or so. Last, but by no means least, can you afford a litter of Airedale puppies? Think – you are going to have to spend a lot of money before you can hope to get anything back and even then you may only break even. So, if you think you want to breed Airedales as a sideline to make money forget about it right now! There will be the cost of the stud fee – from one hundred to two hundred pounds – the cost of extra food and vitamins for your bitch, the cost of a whelping box (unless you are a handyman), the heating, the possible large veterinary bills if the whelping is not straightfor-ward, and lots of money to feed the puppies from three weeks or so up to the time that they are able to go to their new homes, which is eight weeks at the earliest. There is the possibility that some will linger until they are quite a bit older than that and you may have to spend a lot on advertising. All this means a considerable outlay of money and if the job is not done properly the puppies will suffer as a result and could have problems for the rest of their lives. Never was the saying 'you only get out what you put in' more true than when applied to the rearing of Airedale puppies.

Apart from the question of feeding, you must have a good-sized room, or draught-free outbuilding, with access to an outside area that the puppies can play in from the time that they start being able to wander around (at about four weeks of age) until the time that they are sold. If you have a weak stomach and do not like mess, do not breed Airedales because believe it or not, if you have a number of puppies in the litter you will certainly have a lot of mess to clear up! We suggest that you start hoarding newspapers right now.

If you are still determined to breed a litter, think about it well in advance and make sure that your bitch is in good condition, and has been wormed within the few months prior to her season. Try to keep her the correct weight and notice how her seasons proceed. Some bitches have shorter seasons than others and come to their mating time earlier. It will help when you actually come to mate her to know from previous seasons when she is most likely to be ready for mating. Watch her carefully: her vulva should swell up and the bleeding decrease as she gets near the time for mating, and she will twitch her tail from side to side when she is rubbed on her back near the tail. To this end we recommend that you keep her well groomed and tidied up around her rear end. It will be very difficult for you to see much if she is like a hairy doormat in that region. This does not mean that you need go to the lengths that one elderly gentleman did when he brought his bitch to be mated some years ago. He proudly walked her from his car beautifully decked out with a garland of flowers around her neck!

Mating your Bitch

As soon as you have decided that you want to mate your bitch, look around for a suitable dog and contact the owner to see if he agrees to let his dog serve your bitch. He may suggest that you visit him first with her and a copy of her pedigree if she is not a known show specimen. He can then decide whether the combination would be good or not. If he thinks that it will be, he may ask you to let him know as soon as your bitch comes into season so that arrangements can be made for the day or days that will be best for the mating. This is where your monitoring of previous seasons should help as you will be able to suggest when she will be most ready and for how long.

Most bitches can be mated successfully over a period of at least five days from first becoming ready for mating. If she is a maiden bitch, that is if this is the first time she has been mated, it would be as well for her to be served twice with a day or two between each service. Most books will tell you that a bitch should be mated on the tenth and twelfth days, but few Airedales are ready at this time. Indeed some will not conceive unless mated really late in their season, some at seventeen or even nineteen days. Of course there is the odd bitch that has a very short season and is ready on the ninth day. The great Emma, Ch. Ginger Xmas Carol was one of the latter and it was a work of art trying to figure out when to mate her. In the end we left it to her and the chosen dog and they made a very good job of it. That is easy of course when both animals live in the same place.

When you have agreed the day and time to visit the stud dog, make sure that your bitch has had ample exercise before you set off, and has not been fed a large meal. Leave her in the car while you contact the dog's owner as she may cause havoc at the kennel or house. If you have travelled a long distance make sure that you can take your bitch somewhere to relieve herself.

Most stud dog owners have different ways of handling the job but we do like the dog and bitch to have a short time to get to know and flirt with each other before the bitch is held for the dog to mate. If she is very anti and aggressive it will take a lot longer, so allow plenty of time. The reason will probably be because the bitch is afraid, so every effort should be made to calm and reassure her. Most Airedale bitches are co-operative though, if mated on the correct day.

With a good mating the dog and bitch remain tied for a time, varying from ten minutes to half an hour, but a tie is not essential to produce puppies. Some of the shortest matings have produced big litters.

A bitch in season must be carefully watched and kept where no unwelcome visitors can get to her. Labradors appear to be very good at this and seem able to scale great heights to get to bitches in season. We have seen lots of Airedale-Labrador combinations and they are delightful looking creatures but . . .! Years ago a yellow Labrador that lived on a nearby farm always came up to Jokyl when we had a bitch

Jan	Mar	Feb	Apr	Mar	May	Apr	June	May	July	June	Aug	July	Sept	Aug	Oct	Sept	Nov	Oct	Dec	Nov	Jan	Dec	Feb
1	5	1	5	1	3	1	3	1	3	1	3	1	2	1	3	1	3	1	3	1	3	1	2
2	6	2	6	2	4	2	4	2	4	2	4	2	3	2	4	2	4	2	4	2	4	2	3
3	7	3	7	3	5	3	5	3	5	3	5	3	4	3	5	3	5	3	5	3	5	3	4
4	8	4	8	4	6	4	6	4	6	4	6	4	5	4	6	4	6	4	6	4	6	4	5
5	9	5	9	5	7	5	7	5	7	5	7	5	6	5	7	5	7	5	7	5	7	5	6
6	10	6	10	6	8	6	8	6	8	6	8	6	7	6	8	6	8	6	8	6	8	6	7
7	11	7	11	7	9	7	9	7	9	7	9	7	8	7	9	7	9	7	9	7	9	7	8
8	12	8	12	8	10	8	10	8	10	8	10	8	9	8	10	8	10	8	10	8	10	8	9
9	13	9	13	9	11	9	11	9	11	9	11	9	10	9	11	9	11	9	11	9	11	9	10
10	14	10	14	10	12	10	12	10	12	10	12	10	11	10	12	10	12	10	12	10	12	10	11
11	15	11	15	11	13	11	13	11	13	11	13	11	12	11	13	11	13	11	13	11	13	11	12
12	16	12	16	12	14	12	14	12	14	12	14	12	13	12	14	12	14	12	14	12	14	12	13
13	17	13	17	13	15	13	15	13	15	13	15	13	14	13	15	13	15	13	15	13	15	13	14
14	18	14	18	14	16	14	16	14	16	14	16	14	15	14	16	14	16	14	16	14	16	14	15
15	19	15	19	15	17	15	17	15	17	15	17	15	16	15	17	15	17	15	17	15	17	15	16
16	20	16	20	16	18	16	18	16	18	16	18	16	17	16	18	16	18	16	18	16	18	16	17
17	21	17	21	17	19	17	19	17	19	17	19	17	18	17	19	17	19	17	19	17	19	17	18
18	22	18	22	18	20	18	20	18	20	18	20	18	19	18	20	18	20	18	20	18	20	18	19
19	23	19	23	19	21	19	21	19	21	19	21	19	20	19	21	19	21	19	21	19	21	19	20
20	24	20	24	20	22	20	22	20	22	20	22	20	21	20	22	20	22	20	22	20	22	20	21
21	25	21	25	21	23	21	23	21	23	21	23	21	22	21	23	21	23	21	23	21	23	21	22
22	26	22	26	22	24	22	24	22	24	22	24	22	23	22	24	22	24	22	24	22	24	22	23
23	27	23	27	23	25	23	25	23	25	23	25	23	24	23	25	23	25	23	25	23	25	23	24
24	28	24	28	24	26	24	26	24	26	24	26	24	25	24	26	24	26	24	26	24	26	24	25
25	29	25	29	25	27	25	27	25	27	25	27	25	26	25	27	25	27	25	27	25	27	25	26
26	30	26	30	26	28	26	28	26	28	26	28	26	27	26	28	26	28	26	28	26	28	26	27
27	31	27	May 1	27	29	27	29	27	29	27	29	27	28	27	29	27	29	27	29	27	29	27	28
28	Apr 1	28	May 2	28	30	28	30	28	30	28	30	28	29	28	30	28	30	28	30	28	30	28	Mar 1
29	Apr 2			29	31	29	July 1	29	31	29	31	29	30	29	31	29	Dec 1	29	31	29	31	29	Mar 2
30	Apr 3			30	June 1	30	July 2	30	Aug 1	30	Sept 1	30	Oct 1	30	Nov 1	30	Dec 2	30	Jan 1	30	Feb 1	30	Mar 3
31	Apr 4			31	June 2			31	Aug 2			31	Oct 2	31	Nov 2			31	Jan 2			31	Mar 4

Whelping table. First column lists mating date, second column lists whelping date.

43

in season but never otherwise. We could not fathom out how that dog knew.

If you are unlucky enough to have your bitch mismated your veterinary surgeon can give her an injection to negate this but of course you cannot mate her again that season, and sometimes the injection upsets the normal cycle and makes it difficult to get the bitch into whelp next time.

Whelping

The period of gestation is sixty-three days but you must be prepared for the puppies to arrive at least a week early. The bitch must be introduced to her whelping box and the room that she is to whelp in, well in advance. Some pet bitches may not take kindly to being shut away from the family, in which case it would be better to try and arrange for her to be in a position to see the family without having too much disturbance. Wherever she is to whelp must be warm and draught free.

Buy or make a box suitable for the bitch to whelp in, preferably one that can be easily washed. Fit a rail around the inside a few inches from the side and a few inches from the floor – this will help prevent the puppies being crushed by the mother. Put newspaper in the box so that the bitch can scratch it up to make a bed to have her babies in. She will probably tear it up into small pieces but do not be tempted to keep tidying it up as she will get frustrated by having to start all over again. Trim off all the hair from underneath her so that the puppies can get to the teats and also trim the hair off from her rear end and up the back of her tail. This will make it much easier to keep her clean.

The bitch will go off her food prior to whelping and her temperature will drop a few degrees from the normal 101.5F (40.5C). She may also sit looking very uncomfortable and shivery, and from now on needs watching carefully. Make sure that there are plenty of towels handy – old absorbent ones are best – and a hot-water bottle and a cardboard box with some soft towelling.

The bitch will start straining and the contractions will come closer and closer together and stronger until the water bag appears, and then if all goes well the puppy will be born. Each puppy will be born in a transparent sac or 'bag' which contains fluid and is attached to the placenta or afterbirth. The puppy must be removed as quickly as

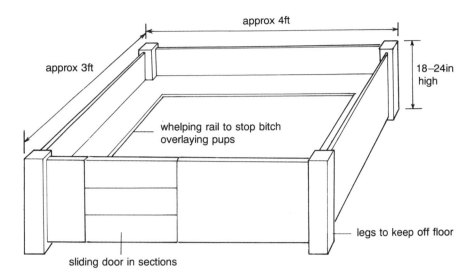

approx 4ft

approx 3ft

18–24in high

whelping rail to stop bitch overlaying pups

legs to keep off floor

sliding door in sections

A suitable whelping box.

possible from the sac or it will drown. If the bitch does not do this, it must be done for her and the puppy wiped around the mouth to remove any excess fluid, and the umbilical cord severed. The puppy must be rubbed dry and this will cause it to open its lungs and start breathing properly.

Usually the bitch will do all this and often resents any interference in which case she should be left to do it as too much fuss may upset her. The puppy should be put to the bitch and encouraged to suckle as this helps promote more contractions.

As more puppies are born the first ones may get scattered or sat on so this is where the cardboard box and hot-water bottle come in. Put the puppies into the box with a towel or cloth over the hot-water bottle and a thin cloth over the top so that they keep warm but do not burn.

Every bitch varies in the time taken between delivering puppies but if more than two hours go by without a puppy being born it is advisable to call in a veterinary surgeon. It could be that there is a puppy which is too big or wrongly presented for the bitch to whelp, or she could have gone into uterine inertia which means that the uterus is failing to contract. In all cases it is wise to call in a professional.

The vet will probably give an injection to induce contractions and as a last resort will do a Caesarean section to remove the puppies. If this is done in time, the puppies will be perfectly all right and so will the dam once she has come round from the anaesthetic. Be careful not to leave her alone with the puppies until you are absolutely sure that she is fully recovered from being anaesthetized or she may accidentally lie on a puppy.

Airedales often have large litters and will get very thirsty. There should always be fresh water available but the bitch quite probably will not want to get out of the whelping box. It is a good idea to offer her small drinks of milk after the birth of three or four puppies. Use goat's milk or milk powder specifically made for dogs and not cow's milk as this can cause scouring.

Make sure that every puppy can feed and is getting some of the precious milk or colostrum as this first milk is called. This first milk is very important for the puppies since it contains vital anti-bodies, and it is also important that the bitch is suckled to promote the milk supply or she will not produce enough for her litter. In a large litter there will undoubtedly be some smaller or weaker puppies and every effort must be made to make sure that they have a chance to get to the milk bars and have a good drink without being pushed away by the bigger pups. The bigger pups can be taken away for short times so that the little ones can get as much as they want to drink. If the milk supply is not that plentiful, the puppies can be bottle fed with a substitute that is widely available and especially produced for bottle-feeding puppies.

The new mother will have to be coaxed away from her puppies so that she can go outside to relieve herself. It is very important that she does this. While she is away, the bed can be cleaned up and some new bedding introduced. There are some very good dog beddings on the market these days and these can be purchased to order in any size. Buy several pieces the exact size of the whelping box so that laundering is no problem. The practicality of this type of bedding becomes clear as it lets the dampness through but the top of the bed stays dry and warm. Also the puppies can get a purchase on it instead of slithering around on paper, which must be better for their little legs.

Quite a few Airedale puppies are born with white on their chests and occasionally with white feet. Do not worry unduly about this as generally speaking it will have grown out on the feet by the time the puppies are eight weeks of age. A little white on the chest is quite all right, as when the dog is trimmed it is usually not at all noticeable. Some of the best dogs we have seen have had some white on the chest.

However well the whelping has gone we think it most advisable to call in a veterinary surgeon to check the bitch over. An antibiotic injection is a good precaution against infection especially if the whelping has been a protracted one.

The new mother will probably need tempting to eat for the first few days and so it is as well to hold the dish for her in the box. Several tasty small meals and milky drinks that she will take right away are better than large meals that she picks at and leaves. Sometimes one has to sit and hold the tasty morsels in one's hand but it is better to do this and get good nourishment into the bitch as soon as possible. She will soon come round to eating well, as long as she is offered food that she fancies.

Puppies are born with their eyes closed and these gradually open at twelve to fourteen days; this is quite exciting as the puppies suddenly seem more like little individuals.

Complications

Keep a careful eye on the bitch after whelping. If she has a dark discharge from her vagina this should be checked by a veterinary surgeon. Also keep an eye on her mammary glands and try to ensure that the puppies suckle from all of them or this could lead to trouble. The glands should be full but supple and any signs of hardening or feeling of heat in them must be treated immediately. If the bitch is making too much milk cut down on her meat and give dry food and plain water to drink until the problem settles down or, if things get worse, she may need antibiotics. Take her temperature and if it is much higher than normal get professional help right away. If she is not making enough milk increase her meat and milk meals and make sure that the pups keep working at her teats to try and promote more. Keep the puppies nails short at all times so that they do not scratch the dam's tummy as this will make her disinclined to stay with them and do her job properly.

Docking Tails and Dew-claws

At present we are still allowed to dock puppies' tails and this should be done at around three days. Some veterinary surgeons refuse to do this and some that will, take off far too much, which spoils the whole look of the dog especially in the show ring. Stand over the veterinary surgeon and make sure that he only takes off the correct amount –

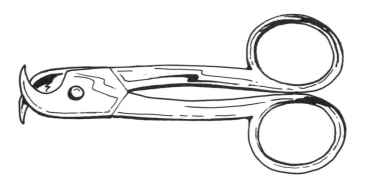

Docking Scissors.

about one third. This is approximate, because the length of tail varies from puppy to puppy. It is best for the tail to be the same length as the neck which is not easy to determine at that age. If you have a breeder nearby who docks his own puppies he may consent to do it for you.

The dew-claws, an extra toe on the front legs, must be removed as well. To dock and dew-claw yourself you will need sterilized docking scissors, small curved scissors and permanganate of potash crystals crushed to a fine powder. When the length of tail to be left has been decided, pull down the skin as much as possible towards the root of the tail and cut firmly. Dip the end of the tail into the permanganate of potash powder to seal the wound. The puppy will hardly squeal. To remove the dew-claws press the scissors under the joint close to the leg and cut the whole joint off. Great care must be taken with this, and in our opinion it is much easier to dock than to dew-claw. Dab on permanganate of potash. We would strongly recommend that you enlist the help of a more experienced breeder. You will definitely need someone to hold each puppy for you as they can be incredibly wriggly even at that age. Try to dock and dew-claw the puppies far enough away from the bitch so that she does not become distressed by their absence – if she can be out on exercise so much the better. When the puppies are all docked and dew-clawed check them over again to make sure that there is no bleeding and put them back with the mother. They will go and start to feed right away and be none the worse for the experience.

5

Puppy Management

The first few weeks of the puppies' lives are spent very lazily, drinking and sleeping, and they grow at a prodigious rate. They should look glossy and firm with fat little tummies. When they get to about three weeks of age they will start moving around more and if the litter is a large one there may be indications that they need supplementary feeding. Sometimes one needs to start even earlier than this, but the older the puppies are the easier it is to teach them to lap and so on. Each puppy should be fed individually so that it is possible to see exactly how much each one is getting. Scraped lean beef is the best starter for puppies – failing this, obtain finely-minced lean beef and mash it to a pulp with a fork and form into individual balls for each puppy. Put some on your finger and put it into the puppies mouths so that they can suck it off. They usually love it. Feed each puppy its portion – you will soon see how well it satisfies them.

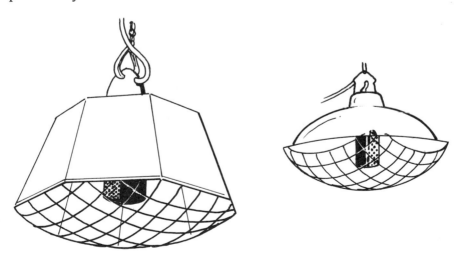

Infra red lamps, which are useful for keeping the whelping bed warm.

Weaning and Early Care

Introducing puppies to lapping can be really messy and again, feeding them one at a time helps in this respect. Put some milk in a saucer and hold it for the puppy, keeping its legs out of the way if possible! Use a milk powder especially manufactured for dogs, as it is less likely to upset their digestions. Gently put the puppy's nose to the milk, and usually they get the idea very quickly. If they do not you can dip your finger into the milk and then into the puppy's mouth. Once it has got the taste it will soon be lapping instead of blowing. At the end of the first few days of weaning the puppies should be having two meals which will take the strain away from their dam. Later on the milk can be made into more of a meal by thickening it with cereal. Alternatively, there are many excellent brands of food that puppies can be weaned on, and they come with full instructions.

Wean the puppies gradually or they will get upset stomachs. Whatever feeding regime is followed, the correct proportions of vitamins, minerals, protein and carbohydrates must be given. Do not try to feed the puppies just after they have been suckling their dam – it is obvious that they will not want what you have to offer. It is quite

Puppies feeding from their dam.

Puppies. Note the fleecy bedding.

surprising though that when one thinks they are full from whatever it may be that they have been offered, as soon as mum comes along they can always manage a drink from her!

At about this time the puppies will be trying to get out of the bed. If the sides are fairly low they will succeed soon enough and it is far safer then to let one side down so that they can run in and out without injuring themselves. The dam will probably want to be away from her puppies for periods of time as they will be very demanding with their needle-like teeth.

Most puppies, especially those from a bitch's first litter, will have roundworms and these must be got rid of. Four weeks is the best time to dose them unless there are reasons to suppose that their health is suffering as a result of worm infestation before this age. It is so important to rid the puppies of worms as the best food and care in the world will be an absolute waste of money and effort if they are infested with these beastly parasites. In late pregnancy the worm larvae that are in the bitch's muscle tissue pass into the bloodstream and lungs,

51

and thence into the placenta and into the puppies. The puppies bring up the larvae and swallow them, where they pass through the stomach and into the intestines. The larvae take three weeks to mature into worms which are passed through the faeces. These faeces are cleaned up by the bitch and the whole cycle starts again. Worming the bitch before mating helps to keep worm infestation to a minimum. It is also clear that the bitch must be wormed after the puppies have been, and again when she has completely finished with her family.

Get the puppies used to being handled and groom them every day if possible. We always use a fine-tooth comb or flea comb and this keeps the coat from becoming dirty and sticky. It also enables you to see if the puppies have any skin or other problems. When they have been groomed from such an early age they take it as a fact of life and should not object to it.

By the time the puppies are five to six weeks of age they should be having four meals a day and if the weather is warm they can go outside for a few minutes to run around and see some new sights.

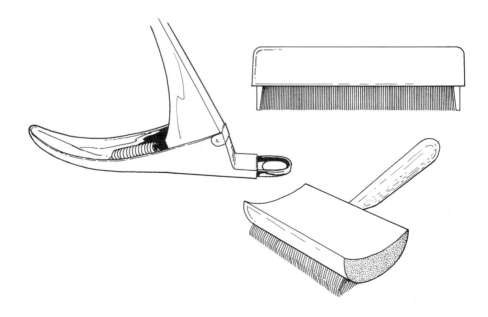

Nail clippers (left), a fine-toothed comb (top) useful for grooming young puppies, and a slicker brush (right) which can be used to groom pups and adult dogs.

When they are indoors their bed must be kept warm and dry. Airedales are very clean dogs and even the puppies soon learn that the bed is not the place to relieve themselves. An infra-red lamp hung over the bed keeps it nicely warm and encourages the puppies to lie in the bed and not on the floor. If they keep dragging the bedding out to play with, use shredded paper as this can be burnt and saves on the laundry bills. Newspapers on the floor are easy to take up and can be burnt or put into plastic sacks for the refuse collectors to take away. It is a good idea to have somewhere to put the puppies while the kennel or room is being cleaned. A portable run is useful as it can be put up inside or outdoors. The bed and everywhere that the puppies go should be thoroughly cleaned and disinfected every day, and dried thoroughly before they are put back. Damp conditions are bad for the development of bones and muscles and also encourage fungi (e.g. ringworm) to thrive.

The puppies are probably costing quite a lot to feed now but it is worth every penny to see sleek, fat, healthy and happy puppies. They are so sweet now, playing and play-fighting with each other and even at this tender age *the* puppy that you have hoped to breed may be

Fifteen pups enjoying their dinner.

showing its style and quality. Four meals a day should be sufficient if the puppies are well and eating up properly.

Gradually allow the mother to be away from her puppies until she does not want to go in with them any more, and her milk will then reduce naturally. Most Airedale bitches like to keep an eye on their puppies to see that they are being looked after properly and the good mothers will bring up their own food for the puppies. This is nothing to worry about and is a natural thing for her to do. However, the trouble is that she will get thinner and the puppies will not want to eat the food that is prepared for them. Make sure that she cannot go into her puppies for several hours after she has been fed so that she will not regurgitate.

Give the puppies toys to play with and make plenty of noise around them so that they will not get too much of a shock when they go to their new homes. Eight weeks is about the right age to let puppies leave home; make sure that each puppy is eating well, has no parasites and a clean coat and skin. Provide each new owner with full instructions for caring for the puppy including a written diet sheet. Give a pedigree, Kennel Club registration if you have it, insurance cover and advice on inoculations. A demonstration on the use of brush and comb would not come amiss either.

Continue with four meals until the puppy is about four months of age, then cut it down to three for a while. At eight to nine months two meals should be sufficient, making sure that the correct balance is still being maintained at all times. Each puppy varies of course and some need more food than others. The puppies usually start to shed their

Trimming nails. With the foot held firmly, cut below the quick to avoid bleeding.

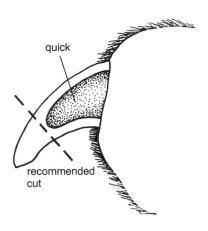

quick

recommended
cut

milk teeth at about three and a half months of age and this continues until they are eight months old. During this time the ears can become very erratic and may need to be stuck in the correct position. If this is the first litter you have bred, seek the advice of a more experienced breeder. To help prevent peculiar ear carriage it is best to keep the hair trimmed on the head and edges of the ears. Four months of age is also a good time to trim off all the puppy leg hair so that the new crisp hair can grow.

Initial Training

If several puppies are running together they may start to fight, generally a good shake and a stern word to the offenders is enough to bring them into line and after a few skirmishes they seem to grow out of it. Airedale Terriers usually get on well together but there are exceptions and if you get a real fighter, you have to run it with one of the opposite sex or only with its own sex when you are there to exercise discipline. Strict training can work wonders with these naughty ones and it could be worth while seeking advice from a trainer used to Airedales if this problem is encountered.

As the puppies grow older they will look for and find all sorts of mischief to get into. They love to chew anything and everything and Airedales are really wonderful diggers. They are like children: they get bored and need something to occupy themselves with. Toys that they cannot chew up, large marrow bones and old slippers that they can play tug-of-war with, will all take their minds off chewing the kennel or wherever they are. Persistent chewers can be deterred by painting bitter apple onto the attractive area. A last resort would be one of the substances which are used to stop horses chewing their stables. These are rather horrible and sticky but usually effective.

The most important things at this age are to make sure that the puppies have room to play and chase around when they want to but have somewhere warm and dry to go to rest. Do not be tempted to walk youngsters for miles, as this is very bad for them and may damage their legs, and in particular their hips. Give them plenty to do and see, and try to socialize them as much as possible. Feed them the correct diet and keep them the right weight – not too fat nor too thin. Always have fresh water available, especially if you are using feeding products that state this.

The ideal kennelling arrangement for puppies is for them to be able to go in and out at will, to enjoy the fresh air and sunshine. A combination of grass and some hard surface, slabs of concrete or stones are good for the run area. It is essential that the area near the gate is slabbed or concreted otherwise it could turn into a mud bath. A good chain link fence dug at least eighteen inches into the ground (how these Airedales love to dig!), and high enough to keep out intruders is required. The kennel should be draught free and preferably constructed of non-chew material.

Electricity should be laid on so that the inside and outside area can be lit and heat provided if necessary. An outside water tap is useful and indeed essential if the run has much concrete or slabbed area so that it is easy to hose down frequently. It also makes it easier to keep the water bowls full. If the puppy is to be shut in the kennel, make sure that he can see out without having to stand on his hind legs or jump up, both of which would be very bad for the formation of his front and back legs. The bed should be raised off the floor and some form of bedding put in, although most Airedale puppies prefer to play with bedding rather than sleep on it.

Trying to decide which puppy to keep can sometimes be very difficult. It is a good idea to watch them running about as much as possible. That way it is much easier to see which puppies have style and are posers, although some do look better running about than they do 'stacked' or held up together on the table. We have already discussed the finer points to look for in Chapter 3. Some people have what is known as a good eye for a puppy – in fact it is quite uncanny how many people who want a puppy purely as a pet pick out the best one – the best in our opinion that is! Conversely many people who have been breeding for years are not good at picking puppies. It does help a lot of course if one knows the line and the generations behind both parents. If there is a type all the way back and one has been able to watch the dogs from puppyhood it is much easier to predict accurately the way the new generation will finally turn out.

Most Airedale puppies are easy to housetrain. The main thing to remember is that if the puppy has been asleep, the first thing it will want to do on waking up is to relieve itself. Therefore it is common sense to put him outside as soon as he wakes up and wants to move around. Go out with him and praise him when he has obliged. He will also need to go out after food or drink, last thing at night and as soon as the family start to move about in the morning. We have had puppies leave us that have been clean in the house after just a few days.

6

Adolescent and Adult Management

Diet

Growing Airedales need a lot of time and attention paid to them if they are to grow into the wonderful-looking animals they they should be. One of the most important contributory factors is good feeding, and the correct diet for each particular dog should be carefully studied. Some dogs do not thrive on a diet which has too much meat and they can get digestive and/or skin troubles. If this happens there are plenty of alternatives to try until one is found to suit. Other dogs much prefer a more vegetarian diet, we have had quite a few lately who favour pasta and vegetables, particularly if flavoured with garlic!

Do not allow a young animal to become too fat – it is probably better for him to be on the lean side rather than the other way. This seems to be of particular importance in relation to hip and other skeletal problems according to Fred L. Lanting in his book on canine hip dysplasia (*Canine Hip Displasia and Other Orthopedic Problems*, Alpine Publications Inc, 1981). He states that although canine hip dysplasia is an hereditary condition, overweight and over-straining the joints in puppy and young adulthood can contribute to hip dysplasia. However, Lanting qualifies this later in the book by stating that as a result of many years of research and experiments in Sweden, it is clear that, 'The cause lies in the genes, but the incidence and severity are to some degree determined by external factors'.

Education and Training

As well as correct feeding, the Airedale Terrier needs to be educated, and plenty of time should be allowed for this. Airedales can be trained to do anything that other breeds can if the methods are correct. Do not try to teach too much at a time. Make it fun and if the puppy does not

The Airedale is a gentle giant.

seem to be able to learn a particular lesson forget about it for a while and try again at some future date.

Young puppies should not be left unsupervised for long periods at a time or they will become bored and get into mischief. Puppies need to be with someone nearly all the time so that they can be house-trained and socialized. No one who is out at work for most of the day should ever buy a puppy or even an older dog. In the wild, dogs were dependent on each other for companionship and survival and are not happy left alone, especially when they are very young.

The puppy must first of all learn its name and the word 'No'. A puppy will learn these very easily because it is at a very receptive age and eager to please its new 'pack'. You must establish right away who is the 'pack leader' or boss and if you have bought a very dominant puppy carry out dominance exercises. It is no good allowing the puppy to do as it likes when he is small and then to have to eradicate

The Airedale Terrier Club of Rushmoor giving a demonstration at the Aldershot Country Fayre of a Group Stay with distractions. Notice the independent one looking the other way! The Club do a lot of demonstrations for charity and the public never cease to be amazed at seeing a dozen or so Airedales doing this exercise. In the Chairman Geoff Grinham's own words 'somehow similar displays with any other breed seem to lack the impact achieved with our wilful clan of Black and Tans'.

these bad habits at a later date. Start training at eight to twelve weeks of age – it is a mistake to wait until later. Titbits are a great help in training, as well as lots of praise and petting. Never hit or slap a dog, especially a puppy, or a nervous or shy dog. Airedales in particular are very sensitive and once they have been badly scared they will never get over it. The same applies to frightening situations. Try to protect your puppy from the possibility of bad scares especially between eight to twelve weeks of age.

Decide before you have a puppy exactly what you will allow it to do and where in the house and garden you will allow it to go. Use baby gates, put plants and ornaments out of reach, temporarily fence off any parts of the garden that are precious until the puppy has learnt where he may or may not go.

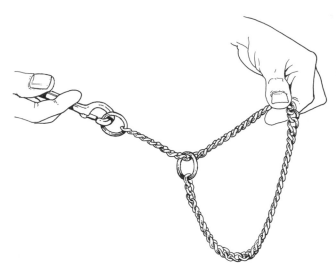

The correct way to put on a training chain.

A good idea might be to have a collapsible cage in which the puppy can rest but still see all that is going on – it will therefore not feel punished when it is put into it. These cages are very easy to erect and dismantle and can be taken anywhere. Put soft bedding and the pup's toys in it and leave the door open to start with, closing it when the puppy is asleep. The puppy and growing dog can be safely put into the cage when visitors come and can be admired but not hurt, and in turn they will not annoy anyone who is not 'doggy'. It is much more friendly than shutting the puppy right away. Make sure though that the cage is not in a draught or in direct sunlight and that the puppy is never left in it for more than two hours at a time. Try to be in the same room as much as possible or the puppy will associate separation anxiety with being in the cage and then of course will not want to go into it. Our dogs love to go into their cages – they probably associate them with a day out at a dog show. As your Airedale puppy grows teach it more and exercise its mind by playing games with it and giving it plenty to think about. You will then gain maximum pleasure from owning an Airedale Terrier.

Remember always to praise and reward good behaviour but to punish bad. If in doubt, ignore whatever it is that the dog has done and he will probably forget it. Be firm but gentle in all your dealings with the puppy so that it will trust you and become confident around people as it grows older. Dogs can only understand the consequences

A lovely Airedale – who could resist a look like that?

of any action that they have taken for a very short while, and so praise or otherwise must come immediately after the action, or it is pointless.

The dog that is kept outside in a kennel needs to have as much human companionship as possible and a routine worked out for him so that he will not become too bored or lonely.

The Airedale's broken coat needs to be kept well brushed and combed to keep it free from dust and dirt. This should be a daily routine and the dog should look forward to and enjoy the experience so much that he jumps onto the grooming table at every opportunity. The hair between the pads should be cut really short with curved scissors because as the hair grows it becomes a solid matt which will be very uncomfortable. Keep the nails filed back. If this is done regularly from puppyhood there should be no problems, and a few treats may even help the dog enjoy it all!

Routines

Try to keep to a routine for feeding and exercising so that the dog will know when to expect food or a run. He will soon learn to tell the time and learn to be clean in his kennel or indoors as a result. As well as plenty of exercise growing dogs and adults need plenty of rest. A dog that is rampaging around all day will not get into the good condition necessary for showing, or on the other hand he may lie down on damp ground which is very bad for him. Raised platforms in the runs are a good idea if the dogs do not demolish them, but even so some dogs prefer to lie on the ground.

The kennels must be cleaned thoroughly every day and at any other time during the day that it may become fouled. Water bowls or buckets should be washed daily and fresh water kept in them all the time. It is most important to check on the water in hot weather as Airedales like to drink a lot, and they also like to dunk their beards in the water and slurp and spray it around. Food bowls must be washed

A walk is twice as enjoyable if shared with a dog.

after each meal and food kept so that flies cannot walk over it or mice nibble at it. Any excreta should be removed right away and the area washed over. Concrete runs should be washed down every day and disinfected, and grass runs should be rested every so often and limed to make sure that they do not become foul. Each dog should be looked over each day and given as much attention as time will allow, especially if he is a kennel dog.

If you have been training your dog on a regular basis his potential as an Obedience dog will be apparent. (We do recommend regular training.) We have had one representative of the breed in her local Obedience team competing at Crufts (Muriel Carrott's Anna) and there are no good reasons why we should not have more. In many other countries especially in America, Australia and Russia, Airedale enthusiasts are really keen on Obedience competitions. We have also found that they do enjoy the Agility exercises and if you are fit and reasonably young this is a great sport. The Airedale Terrier also has a good nose and can be a fine hunter. So far in this country we have only one Airedale Terrier Training Club but hopefully we will have more in the years to come. Most Airedale Terriers are good guardians of their own family and property but this trait is not developed to such a high degree that they would be dangerous. The Airedale is an intelligent and discriminating breed of dog.

Colonel Richardson in his book *Forty Years with Dogs* (Hutchinson) has some marvellous memories of the Airedales that he had trained for the First World War and for watch-dogs. It appears that even in Russia at that time Airedales were being used as messenger dogs, as the trainers apparently preferred them to other breeds and their records were 'certainly greatly superior'. Today the Airedale Terrier is a very popular breed of dog in Russia because of his pleasant character. One of our old dogs 'Jack' (Ch. Jokyl Spaceleader) retired to be a house pet and on one occasion he was left to look after the house with the door left open to the yard. Some time later Jack's owner came back to find the man who had delivered the oil for the central heating, standing in the yard unable to move. Jack had allowed him to enter the yard but there was no way he would let him leave!

As your Airedale Terrier becomes older so do all his working parts and he still needs to be examined carefully and regularly to keep him in good condition. The most obvious parts are his teeth and these need looking after just as your own teeth do. Chewing bones does help a little but the only bones that can be allowed to any dog are large beef bones and chewing these can lead to broken teeth. Large pieces of tough meat in the food can help in cleansing the teeth by removing the collected deposits of bacteria. Regular brushing two or three times a week with special doggy toothpaste keeps the teeth and gums healthy and your dog's breath as fresh as when he was a puppy. If deposits do build up on the teeth these can be removed by scaling, but this should be done by an experienced person or vet. On no account should the calculus be left on the teeth, as this will lead to tooth decay and gum disease, quite apart from the unpleasant odours that will be given off.

As dogs get older they seem to get more greedy! Do not be tempted to give in too often to pleading looks or your dog will become overweight and this is not a kindness to him. Obese dogs are prone to respiratory, heart, liver and joint problems. They are also more likely to have skin and enteric problems, diabetes and stand more chance of premature death. If you are unable to keep your dog's weight down there are special obesity diets, and these can be obtained from a veterinary surgeon.

The time may come when you have to leave your dog for some reason. There are lots of boarding kennels, but it would be a good idea

The 'Rolls Royce' of terriers.

Here Aus. Ch. Windview Ikabod CD, owned by Edwin and Marlene Jacobs, competes at an Agility competition in Perth, Western Australia.

for you to do your own research to find the one best suited to your dog. When you have decided on a kennel, leave the dog there for a few days at a time over a period so that he knows what to expect and knows that you have not abandoned him but will come and collect him sometime.

Whatever you want from your Airedale, whether he is to be a show dog, to be trained to compete in Obedience or Agility, or as a guard and companion treat him with respect and affection and he will repay you over and over again. Remember that the way your dog behaves is to a very high degree a reflection of your own character and the way that you have treated him.

7

The Airedale as a Companion

Pets have always played a great part in the everyday activities of humans. Dogs in particular fulfil many roles as guards or hunters but generally they are companions in the everyday activities of their owners. Without pets life for many older people would be empty, and countless children have learnt lessons in tolerance and loyalty from their dogs. In the early days of the breed, possibly even more than today, Airedales made a very valuable contribution to the lives of their owners. Apart from their more obvious duties as guard dogs, they played an important part in the leisure pursuits of the men. Nowadays we see the Airedale as an essential member of the family. His size and stature make him a formidable guard-dog and his love of children

Dinner for two.

means that their safety is assured. Stories abound of his courage in tackling intruders to protect home or family, and his intelligence when faced with unusual situations. Being a true Terrier (and therefore an earth dog) he can exhibit some of their less desirable traits e.g. he is a natural tunneler. If you are an enthusiastic gardener, give him his own area and discourage his help in yours. In the high hills and lonely places the Airedale comes into his own – he is an outside dog and in his element climbing about amongst the crags and scree. We have always found a walk to be twice as enjoyable if shared with one of our dogs. Some like it more than others but all seem to find pleasure in the great outdoors. A proper Airedale is of course, an independent fellow and this fact should be remembered when planning walks or outings.

Because of his lupine ancestry a dog is essentially an animal used to living in a pack or group with acceptance of a pecking order built into his thinking. This means that he fits easily and successfully into the family structure and gives strong and enduring loyalty to his people. The Airedale Terrier can be inspired to a fealty and devotion which could teach a lesson to many humans. This relationship between man and dog works both ways of course as organizations such as Pat Dogs in the UK and similar bodies in the United States and elsewhere have shown. The old and sick can often benefit both physically and mentally from the presence of a sympathetically orientated dog. Pat Dogs arranges for suitable dogs to be taken to visit patients in hospitals and old people's homes. Our own experience has been that patients look forward eagerly to such visits and hospital staff confirm the beneficial effects of such contacts. The dogs seem to sense the very human need for companionship and reassurance, reacting in the only way that they know: with friendly comfort.

There are many other fields in which our Airedale excels and often these are areas where the natural intelligence, strength and character of the dog enable him to carry out quite demanding tasks. The different skills, many of which are inherent in his ancestral make-up, allow him to carry out many jobs calling for courage, quick-wittedness and fortitude. As we have already said, the Airedale Terrier is second to none as a guard-dog and properly trained he can be a pretty formidable customer. The qualities that are necessary for this work are those which made him such a successful police and war-dog. A certain independence of mind, however, is reputed to have weighed against him with police forces who preferred the more predictable German Shepherd Dog, although the Japanese police are still using Airedales for their police dogs. Contrary to the accepted belief that the Airedale's

An Airedale pulling his weight.

natural and inherent independence made him a difficult subject for the obedience trainer, it has recently been shown that with the right teacher he can be enthusiastically co-operative.

Special Skills

In the south of England, there is a specialist training club for Airedales called the Airedale Terrier Training Club of Rushmoor which aims to enhance the day to day enjoyment of both dog and owner. The Airedale Terrier can also be trained to a high degree of skill in tasks normally performed by other breeds. In the United States at the present time a great effort is being made to test the Airedale Terrier to the limit of his skills. In addition to Agility, Airedales have been taught to flush birds from cover and to retrieve them. The dogs are also taught the basics of racoon hunting and in New South Wales opossum hunting is a further skill. At a recent American workshop, it was seen that dogs with obedience training proved more adaptable in activities that required greater skill, indicating that a disciplined dog can cope more readily with new experiences. In Germany and Finland the Airedale must pass a working test before it can be granted Championship Status.

In the water events, the Airedale's ancestry as a Waterside Terrier, with his double waterproof coat, have stood him in good stead. Another area into which Airedale enthusiasts have ventured is Agility, which is in essence an obstacle race for dogs. In this the Airedale Terrier performs with panache, obviously enjoying the challenge of the various obstacles.

While the increasing urbanization of the UK mitigates against the widespread use of the Airedale's natural and inherited outdoor skills, overseas it is quite another story. The Airedale Terrier has been used frequently in the broader landscapes of other countries as a hunter and tracker.

Along the Yorkshire riverbanks of course his skill against vermin was well-known and in the early years of the breed the otter was hunted successfully. Nowadays however, there would be a justifiable national outcry if this endearing British native mammal were to be harried and hunted. Over the past thirty years the otter population has declined dramatically and this animal is an endangered species today. The otter may disappear entirely by the end of the century if protective measures are not taken. It would certainly not be appreciated if we

'All aboard the Skylark!'

encouraged our Airedales to try and recapture these particular old skills.

If we cross the Atlantic to the United States there is quite a different picture and stories abound of his hunting prowess. The American Kennel Gazette of January 1938 states that 'the Airedale is the most useful of all dogs for all climates'. The smaller terriers and short-coated hounds become more or less unworkable under the terribly severe winter conditions of northern Canada. The article goes on to detail instances of the hunting and outdoor abilities of the Airedale Terrier. Anybody who is in any doubt of the dog's skill as a ratter can see a picture of a proud Airedale bitch, Swiss Mountain Maid with a line of thirty-two rats dug out and killed in just two hours. This of course is one of the original Airedale Terrier areas of expertise in his native Yorkshire. The old breed had a good nose and loud voice. Most Airedale owners would agree about the loud voice – one often hears the word 'mouthy' used to describe a dog.

Ratting in Yorkshire or New Jersey, working the trap lines of frozen North Ontario or opossum hunting in New South Wales all required a strong sense of smell. It is ironic that in the country of his origin the Airedale is in danger of losing his hunting skills because of a lack of

An Airedale having fun in the snow.

opportunity while overseas there is fuller scope for his talents. In the United States there are a wide range of work skills being taught to the Airedale; particularly those of putting up game and retrieving and other outdoor pursuits. In a delightful piece by Harry Wooheuter, *The Memoirs of a Game Ranger*, Biddy, an Airedale Terrier bitch, and her skill in following the spoor of lions in Southern Africa is described. Biddy lived in the Kruger National Park in the early twentieth century and was so skilled that even spoor over twenty-four hours old was easily tracked. Biddy's only fault was over excitement causing a low-pitched whimpering which she seemed quite incapable of controlling and this often warned off the lions and they would escape.

Getting Along with Neighbours

It is essential that your Airedale is not antisocial: one of the quickest ways to achieve unpopularity among your neighbours is to have a dog with bad habits that are not controlled. In urban areas there are many ways to make certain that you and your Airedale stay friends with your friends. In the countryside conditions are somewhat different but

The versatile Airedale – 'I do'.

the rules remain basically the same. Nowadays in towns there are strict laws about fouling areas used by children and adults alike and it is quite essential that these laws be observed. The *Toxocara Canis* round-worm occurs in very many young puppies who receive the larvae from the mother before birth and those larvae then develop into adult worms within fourteen days. It is therefore important that a strict worming programme be carried out at this early stage of the puppies' development. It is advisable to make quite certain, when buying a puppy, that it has been wormed at least twice. In fact it is only by strict adherence to an approved worming programme that you can keep the dog free from infestation: this means multiple dosing to eliminate faecal eggs. It is your responsibility as a dog owner to carry a plastic bag or a scoop to clean up after your dog. It would appear that 11–13 per cent of dogs, excluding young puppies, shed *Toxocara Canis* eggs into the environment. You and your Airedale should not be irresponsible and cause anyone to catch this awful disease.

Did someone say walkies?

Why walk when you can ride?

In urban areas it is vital that the peace and privacy of neighbours is respected. Your dog must not threaten either humans or other animals. Should he be openly aggressive then he must be kept under firm control. The continually barking dog can be as annoying to dog lovers and non dog lovers alike as is the persistent crying of a fractious child. It can be a nuisance under law to offend your neighbour's peace with a noisy dog and simple consideration should govern your dog's behaviour. Dogs who invade a neighbour's property and chase or harm any other animal or bird can be restrained under law. Dogs in the country must be kept under control on a lead. Great care should be exercised so that your dog does not disturb, damage or destroy the burrow, den, set or lair of any wild animal. The dog must not disturb, catch, injure or destroy any bird, fish, reptile or animal. The Country Code must be observed. Those who farm near large urban areas are quite regularly plagued by uncontrolled dogs from towns who worry their livestock. Nothing is more infuriating to the countryman than to find dogs running sheep or cattle often with disastrous results. Many a farmer has pulled the trigger first and left the questions to come later. The law in this area is quite explicit about the burden of proof, but it is much easier all round just to keep the dog out of trouble.

Fun at the seaside.

A dog can be a fine friend and companion if he behaves in a reasonably decorous way but antisocial conduct just makes him into a nuisance to everybody.

8

Showing

The young Airedale has now been reared successfully and if the show bug has bitten, you will be anxious to get him to a show to see how he performs. Most dog exhibitors take at least one of the dog papers and the particulars of all forthcoming shows are to be found in their advertising pages. The name and address of the show secretary and the date, time and venue of the show as well as the closing date for entries will be in the advertisement. Write to the show secretary, and ask for a schedule. This schedule has all the necessary information for an entry to be made and an entry form is always enclosed in the schedule. Read it very carefully and take care to fill in the entry form correctly. Make sure that your dog is registered and has been transferred into your name. It is important that all the details given on the entry form are the same as those recorded on the registration certificate. It has been known for a dog to be disqualified because of one letter being missed out on the entry form! Starting off at a few local shows will help you to gain confidence and give you and your dog practice. Listed below are the types of shows that you can go to, and their definitions.

Matches

Matches are held by some clubs, and are very sociable and relaxing occasions. They are a good way to get young dogs used to being handled and accustomed to other breeds. It is necessary for the judge to handle a dog in order to check his conformation. The judging is on a knockout basis with just two dogs in the ring at a time, and the winner going forward to the next round and so on until there are only two unbeaten dogs left. The winner is then 'Best in Match'. The competition at these Matches can be very strong with top breeders taking their good stock to gain confidence and practice. This is a good opportunity to learn a little about other breeds and meet new and often very knowledgeable people. The Matches are sometimes against other clubs, which makes the competition even more keen and the

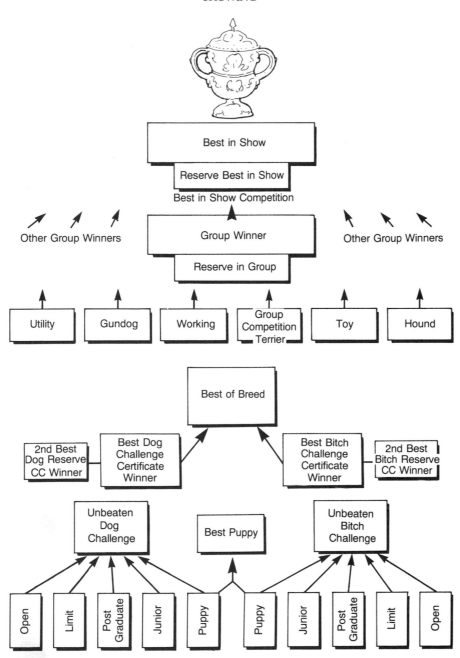

The UK show system.

whole occasion is a very friendly, members-only event with refreshments thrown in.

Exemption Shows

Exemption shows are open to registered and unregistered dogs. Entries do not have to be made in advance; the fees are taken on arrival at the show. There are four classes for registered dogs only and other classes have titles like: the dog with the curliest tail, the dog with the most appealing expression, the dog that the judge would most like to take home and so on. These shows are usually held for a charity or breed rescue societies and are also good schooling for youngsters.

Sanction Shows

Sanction shows never have more than twenty-five classes, the highest being Post Graduate. There are no benching facilities at Sanction shows and so it is possible to leave as soon as you wish after judging has finished. To show at one of these, one has to be a member of the society holding the show.

Limited Shows

Limited shows are also restricted to members of the club. As at Sanction Shows, no dog that has won a Challenge Certificate may compete but the competition can be very strong. There are usually several breeds classified as well as variety classes.

Open Shows

Open shows are as the name implies open to all dogs – champions and novices alike. This makes for very strong competition and is an ideal chance to see how your dog and your presentation compares to that of the more experienced exhibitors. These are probably the best shows for the beginner to attend as there are usually well-known exhibitors attending, from whom much can be learnt even by just watching and observing the handling and trimming techniques.

The classification at Open shows is usually generous with Puppy and Novice classes included, so be sure to enter your dog in as low a class as he is eligible for. Often new exhibitors enter in the Open class without realizing that this is the very class that will contain the best

Judge and exhibitors at the National Terrier Show 1963.

dogs and this can prove a very disappointing beginning. At many Open shows the dogs are required to be benched in their own numbered bench with a collar and lead or chain. The alternative to this is a cage that will fit onto the bench and allow the dog to be seen by the public. Another Kennel Club rule states that 'No dog shall be absent from its bench for more than fifteen minutes'.

The cages can be bought at any Championship and some Open shows, and are collapsible. It does mean that the dog can be fastened in the cage so that no one can interfere with him, and the dog can rest more peacefully and not get tangled with his lead or chain. Airedales have a lively nature and will bounce around to greet anyone who passes their bench and expend a lot of energy before going into the ring. It is surely better to save that energy for showing off to the judge.

Championship Shows

Championship shows are open to all exhibitors and are the most important of all. At most Championship shows there are Challenge Certificates on offer – one for the best dog and one for the best bitch. These large cards, 'CCs' or 'tickets' as we call them, are white with a wide green border and green writing which says 'I am clearly of the opinion that . . . owned by . . . is of such outstanding merit as to be worthy of the title of Champion'. It is everyone's ambition to win these cards.

There are also smaller cards which are Reserve Challenge Certificates or Reserve CCs and they state that the dog or bitch is of sufficient merit to be worthy of being awarded the Challenge Certificate, should the Challenge Certificate winner be disqualified. These are awarded to the dog and bitch that the judge thinks are second best in the breed. Should the CC winner be disqualified for any reason the Reserve CC winner will then become the CC winner. The judge has it within his power to withhold prizes and even the CC if he considers there to be no dog worthy of winning. This does not happen very often. The certificate that is handed out in the ring is not the official one. That comes some one month later when all the particulars of the winner have been found to be in order – it is a very large and grand certificate. When the dog has three Challenge Certificates, under three different judges, he is given the title of Champion and the Kennel Club will send a certificate to that effect in due course. The value of any dog or bitch with the title of Champion is enhanced and so also is the value of their progeny, but for most of us the main pleasure in winning is the thrill of having brought the animal up to the peak of condition, showmanship and trimming.

The following are the definitions of the classes at shows as issued by the Kennel Club, although not every show provides all these classes. Breed Championship shows tend to put on more classes than All-Breed shows as only a few of these classes qualify a dog for exhibition at Crufts show.

Classes and Their Definitions, for Championship and Open Shows

MINOR PUPPY	For dogs of six and not exceeding nine calendar months of age on the first day of the show.
PUPPY	For dogs of six and not exceeding twelve calendar months of age on the first day of the show.
JUNIOR	For dogs of six and not exceeding eighteen calendar months of age on the first day of the show.

BEGINNERS	For owner, handler or exhibit not having won a first prize at Championship or Open show.
MAIDEN	For dogs that have not won a Challenge Certificate or a first prize at an Open or Championship show (Minor Puppy, Special Minor Puppy, Puppy and Special Puppy classes excepted, whether restricted or not).
NOVICE	For dogs that have not won a Challenge Certificate or three or more first prizes at Open and Championship shows (Minor Puppy, Special Minor Puppy, Puppy and Special Puppy classes excepted, whether restricted or not).
TYRO	For dogs that have not won a Challenge Certificate or five or more first prizes at Open and Championship shows (Minor Puppy, Special Minor Puppy, Puppy and Special Puppy classes excepted, whether restricted or not).
DEBUTANT	For dogs that have not won a Challenge Certificate or a first prize at a Championship show (Minor Puppy, Special Minor Puppy, Puppy and Special Puppy classes excepted, whether restricted or not).
UNDERGRADUATE	For dogs that have not won a Challenge Certificate or three or more first prizes at Championship shows (Minor Puppy, Special Minor Puppy, Puppy and Special Puppy classes excepted, whether restricted or not).
GRADUATE	For dogs that have not won a Challenge Certificate or four or more first prizes at Championship shows in Graduate, Post Graduate, Minor Limit, Mid Limit, Limit and Open classes, whether restricted or not.
POST GRADUATE	For dogs that have not won a Challenge Certificate or five or more first prizes at Championship shows in Post Graduate, Minor Limit, Mid Limit, Limit and Open classes, whether restricted or not.
LIMIT	For dogs that have not won three Challenge Certificates under three different judges or seven or more first prizes in all, at Championship shows in Limit and Open classes,

81

	confined to the breed, whether restricted or not, at shows where Challenge Certificates were offered for the breed.
OPEN	For all dogs of the breeds for which the class is provided and eligible for entry at the show. Wins in variety classes do not count when entering in breed classes, but when entering for variety classes, wins in both breed and variety classes must be counted.

Puppies under six months of age are not eligible to be shown except at Exemption shows. Crufts is the show that everyone has heard of so a win here is really prestigious and much sought-after. Visitors come from all over the world to view the dogs at Crufts so there is much interest generated. To be able to be shown at Crufts a dog must have won one of the following: first, second or third prize in Minor Puppy, Puppy, Junior, Post Graduate, Limit or Open class at a Championship Show where there are Challenge Certificates on offer. Any dog who has a Stud Book number is eligible to compete at Crufts Dog Show.

Crufts has always been held in London but in 1991 (the centenary of the show) it was held in Birmingham owing to circumstances beyond the control of the Kennel Club. It had fast been outgrowing Earls Court and the move to the National Exhibition Centre in Birmingham means that more dogs will be eligible to compete. In the 'good old days' there were no qualifying classes and it was grand to see the new puppies that breeders had been bringing on to astound the rest of the fancy. The puppy classes were often the most exciting ones at the show because of this.

Which Show?

There are a number of Airedale Terrier Breed Clubs in the United Kingdom who hold Championship shows and all of them hold Open or Limited shows. These clubs are country wide so somewhere near you is a club that you can join to show your Airedale Terrier against other Airedales and meet other enthusiasts. There is also a club for the whole country called The National Airedale Terrier Association and they hold their shows in different parts of the country each year.

When a suitable show has been found by perusing the dog papers, and the schedule and entry form received, great care must be taken to

Happiness is winning Best in Show at Crufts.

enter the most appropriate classes. The lowest possible is sensible for this first show and not more than two or three classes – it is not a good idea to tire youngsters by showing them in too many classes. Airedale Terriers do get bored quite quickly and so it is far better to make the shows something to be enjoyed rather than endured.

Entries close for All Breed Championship shows six weeks or so beforehand and for Open and Breed shows two to three weeks; other shows about two weeks beforehand. This gives one time to put the finishing touches to the presentation.

Some shows issue passes to get into the venue. Make sure that this is taken on the day and put where it is easy to reach or difficulties and delays will be encountered at the entrance. Keep the pass as it could be needed to get out of the venue as well!

Preparation

The day before the show get together all the equipment that you will need at the show and check on transport arrangements. Top up with petrol etc. so that there will be no unnecessary delay on the journey. Keep a bag especially for the show gear. In it you will need a dolling up pad (a flexible rubber pad with wire pins for brushing up the furnishings), a brush for polishing, a hound glove, a wide-toothed comb and some colourless hair dressing cream or spray to give the final shine. Kennel Club rules state that 'No substance which alters the colour, texture or body of the coat may be used in the preparation of a dog for exhibition either before or at the show'. Take a bowl for food and water and a couple of show leads. These items can be bought at all Championship shows. We use thinnish show leads about $1/2$in (6cm) wide and tough enough to hold a strong dog. Even so accidents can happen and it is wise to have a spare. It will also be nice for the dog if he has a blanket or rug to sit on in the bench, cage or box. A safe collar and lead to walk him is needed, and can be used to fasten him on the bench if he is to be benched. We always take drinking water from home so that there is no chance of our dogs being upset by a change.

It might be as well to take a stripping knife in case there are a few hairs to be trimmed off at the last minute although it is hoped that all that will have been done at home. If your dog shows to bait, take that with you as well. As you can see the list of one's needs get longer, and we usually leave the show bag packed ready from show to show, so there is less likelihood of forgetting anything.

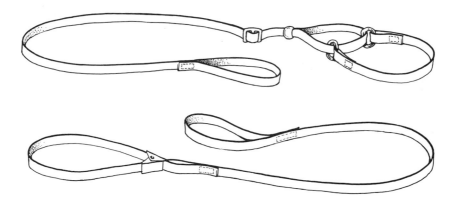

Show leads.

It is a good idea to have your own table and grooming arm: there are many types and a table that collapses and has wheels is very useful especially if you are going to take a cage or box into the show for the dog to sleep in. We must point out again that at benched Championship shows the dog must be in full view of the spectators while on the bench but as long as the box or cage has the top and front of wire mesh the dog can be seen. Take a couple of soft towels as well in case your dog is one who dribbles when he is travelling or if, like most Airedales, he gets his beard in a mess when drinking. A few small plastic bags or a scoop are useful as well so that any motions the dog may pass in or near the show ground can be removed. Do not give any food before setting out unless he is an absolutely marvellous traveller – even dogs who normally travel well can get upset if the traffic is stopping and starting. Winding round bends can also have a very upsetting effect. If necessary, take a small meal to feed on arrival. Another essential item is something to fasten the ring number to your person with – these can be purchased at shows. Alternatively put an elastic band around the left arm to slip the card under.

Make sure that plenty of time is allowed for travelling to the show so that you are not arriving minutes before you are due to go into the ring. Apart from the fact that you will be parked a long way from the entrance if you are late, you will also find a lot more people there queueing to get through the entrance.

Check that your pass is in a handy place so that you do not have to waste time searching for it. When you have found your bench and organized yourself, go and buy a catalogue so that you can work out roughly at what time you will be judged. Locate the ring so that when the class is called you can go straight to it. Locate a suitable place to put up the table – ,there are usually specially designated areas for grooming, and choose one as near to the ring as possible. This is wise advice as it is the responsibility of each exhibitor to get into his class on time. The ring steward only has the responsibility of telling exhibitors that judging is about to commence; he cannot round up the exhibitors for each class.

When the dog has been exercised, put him on the table, brush and comb him and trim off any hairs that have grown since the last trim – they will have grown even if it was only the previous day that he looked perfect! Check that his eyes are clean and his beard dry. If judging is not to be for a while put him in his box, cage or bench for a rest and tend to your own needs. Make sure that you are looking neat and tidy; it is an insult to the dog and the judge for exhibitors not to look as well turned out as possible. Dress to complement the dog – not too flashy, but certainly not scruffy.

In the Ring

When the time approaches for the judging of the class for which you have entered, make sure that you and your dog are ready – give the final polish and go into the ring. The ring steward will tell you where to stand and give you your ring card if they are not on the bench – remember this has to be displayed where it can be seen easily. The judge will look at the dogs when they are standing in line. Pose your dog and try to get him to make a good impression on the judge. He will then probably ask all the exhibits to walk round the ring at least once and there again make sure that your dog is on his best behaviour, head held high without him being strangled, and stepping out correctly. Make sure the dog is on your inside (your left) – it is usual to be moved anti-clockwise and as the judge stands in the middle of the ring, he must be able to see the dogs moving without the hindrance of human legs.

When the judge has seen the dogs move round he will call the first one into the ring to 'go over'. This means that he will examine the dog thoroughly, and this is where the early training will pay off as the dog must stand still and allow the judge to touch him all over without backing off or trying to bite.

When the examination is completed, the judge will ask the handler to move the dog, probably in a triangle. This means walking away

English and Swedish Champion Jokyl Hot Lips – After a successful career in England Hot Lips became the top winning Airedale in Sweden in 1984. 'Winnie' lives with her owner in an apartment, proving that Airedale Terriers can be companions and show dogs at the same time.

from the judge, dog on your left, turning left and walking across the ring, turning left again towards the judge, keeping the judge in view out of the corner of your eye so that you actually do walk towards him. If your dog walks well on a loose lead with head and tail up this is very good. If he does not, make sure to get the lead well up the throat and just behind the ears (do not pull it up so tightly that the dog is choked nor yet so loose that you have no control over him). Previous practice will have got you both used to the best speed to move for the smoothest gait.

After moving, each dog will go back into line again until the judge has seen every exhibit go through his paces. Keep an eye on the judge so that you know when the last dog is being examined. Make sure the dog's leg hair and whiskers are neat and tidy and that he is standing properly: front legs together, hind legs out behind him, head and tail held high and right up on his toes.

The judge will then probably walk along the line-up of dogs to have another look at heads, expressions, coat texture, general outline and appearance before pulling four or five into the centre of the ring for a

Swedish Champion Jokyl Top Hat 'n' Tails s. Ch. Jokyl Smart Guy, d. Ch. Jokyl Buttons 'n' Bows. Top winning dog in Sweden and sire of many winners and winners of progeny classes. Owned by Gunnel Lindberg and Susanne Sparre (handling). See how well he is standing, on his toes and not needing to be propped up.

final look over and sometimes another check on movement. He will then place them in his order of preference from left to right, mark his judging book and ask a ring steward to hand out the prize cards. A steward will ask the first and second to stay in the ring while the judge writes or dictates a report.

Any dogs that are in a subsequent class will be placed on one side of the ring by a steward in the order that they were placed in the previous class. They will join the new dogs when they have been looked at by the judge and the class will progress as before.

If you are lucky enough to win the class you must be ready to go into the challenge. This takes place after the Open class, and all unbeaten dogs compete for the Best of Sex. If it is a Championship show and the Open class winner has won the Challenge Certificate, the second in the Open class will be called in to challenge for the Reserve Challenge Certificate. The best dog and best bitch will then compete for Best of Breed.

After the judging you will be either delighted or disappointed with what you have achieved at this first show. Whatever the outcome

An Airedale correctly set up to show.

though, remember that it is a sport and accept the results gracefully. Remember that there is always another show. You will be meeting and making friends with some really super people and hopefully gaining as much pleasure from showing (win or lose) as we have done over the years.

9

Show Preparation

Long before you enter for a show you should start preparing your dog, both in mind and body, and this takes more than the few weeks that elapse after the entries have closed – in fact we would recommend getting the dog absolutely right and then looking for a show.

Patience is definitely the name of the game here. The Airedale is a very sensitive dog and any wrong treatment can affect the temperament – often irreversibly – so go slowly and patiently through your preparation. You should already have your dog used to being on the table for brushing and combing and so once the inoculations are

A well-trimmed head.

*Ch. Jokyl Smartie Pants – held the bitch record for winning the
highest number of CCs (18) in 1976. Has produced a record
number of English champions. This untouched photograph shows
how the trimmed dog should look.*

finished with, try to get your puppy out into the world. Take it slowly
at first so that he can get used to the traffic gradually. Going into pubs
is a good way to get youngsters used to people as nearly everyone in
a pub likes to make a fuss of a dog. This is wonderful because then
the youngsters grow to have faith in strangers and will not shy away
from judges in the ring.

Our oldest dog, Cedric, still loves to go pub crawling and he is so
well known up at the local that his weakness (chocolate bars) is
pandered to and he virtually has them lined up on the bar. Amazingly
he still has all his teeth but he does have to go on a diet every now
and again!

Before you take your youngster out on the road you should already
have taught him how to walk up and down properly at home. Some
youngsters buck and leap and others dig their toes in, tail down and
refuse to budge. The rare one will take to the lead like a duck to water
and this one will probably be a natural showman. The reluctant
movers will have to coaxed and 'jollied' along with the aid of titbits

and making a game of it all. The Airedale is a happy creature so everything that is fun is usually accepted as OK!

Do not force the issue at this stage. If your Airedale really learns to hate the lead you could have a problem for a long time to come. Try a little training at a time – coaxing and rewarding – this way the dog will learn to enjoy his outings on a lead. The too-exuberant dog will gradually learn to walk properly. Fish him around on the lead and if he is really bold a few sharp tugs on the lead will not hurt him. As long as you are talking to him all the time, praising and petting, he will soon realize what you want him to do and aim to please you.

Above all it must be an enjoyable exercise. Do not worry if it seems to be taking time – remember – be patient! As he grows into the idea of lead work teach him to stand properly. This can be best achieved if he is interested in something a little way off as you can place his legs in the right position without his noticing and getting upset about it. After a while he will get used to it and not bother over much and will automatically stand himself and show off.

Showmanship

Some Airedales are natural show offs and this should be encouraged. It is so much easier to handle a dog who is a natural showman, not to mention the fact that he must catch the judge's eye more than something that has to be 'stacked' up and held together. These showy dogs can make anyone look a good handler but even so they still do have to be handled properly to look their best.

If your dog is not one of these naturals you will have to find something to make him come alive in the ring or he could be overlooked in favour of a less good specimen that is really showing his head off. Most dogs perk up for liver, cheese or even chocolate but you have to practise at home a lot so that your dog can learn to look at the bait and not leap all over you to devour it! Never throw your bait over the ring to attract your dog as this can be distracting to the other exhibits and is therefore unfair. The same is true of squeaky toys which can be a real nuisance for other exhibitors if over used – the idea is to help your own dog show but not to sabotage the showmanship of the other exhibits.

Some dogs show off very well at home but when they get into the ring they either spook or stand looking and acting as if they are bored stiff. All of one's patience comes into play to try and coax him to perform properly; you will have to do the best you can and help him along and hope that after a few shows he will get used to it and relax and enjoy it all. This is where all your early training and socializing should pay off.

Stripping and Trimming

We have written previously about feeding and hopefully you have settled on a diet that suits your dog and he is really fit with a good firm body – not thin and not overweight. He should be getting some good exercise – a combination of free running and lead work is perfect if you can manage it. We will assume that you have been keeping the

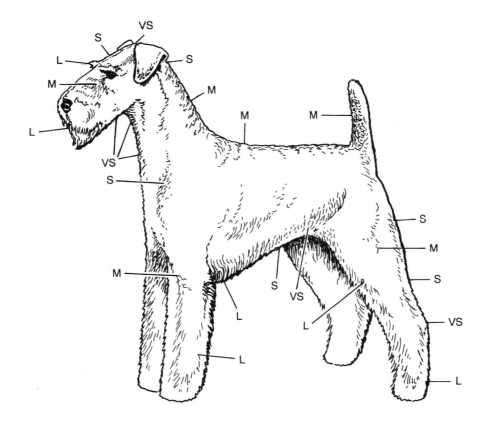

A trimming chart. Key: short – S, very short – VS, medium length – M, long – L.

A grooming arm.

coat well combed so that it is now ready to be stripped. We do not propose to try and explain hair by hair how to trim a dog for show as that could take a whole volume of words and pictures. Instead we will try and explain the basics and the rest you must learn by practising, by studying the trimming of those exhibitors that you think do a good job of presentation, by asking the more experienced (but not when they are minutes away from going into the ring!) and in general by trying to pick up all you can to help yourself. Trimming can be taught and we would say that anyone can learn to strip a dog if they want to, but to be able to show-trim a dog to make it look really good you must have a flair for it, and a good eye for detail. Keep in your mind a picture of what the finished animal should look like. Never try to trim too much without pausing often to look at what you have done.

Before attempting to strip the hair from your dog a few basic tools are necessary:

Stripping knife Choose one that is comfortable to hold and not too sharp – a sharp knife in inexperienced hands can have the same effect as clippers. Most are manufactured for right- or left-handed people so be sure to get the correct one.

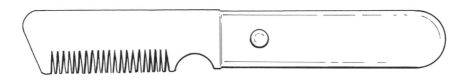

A stripping knife/rake.

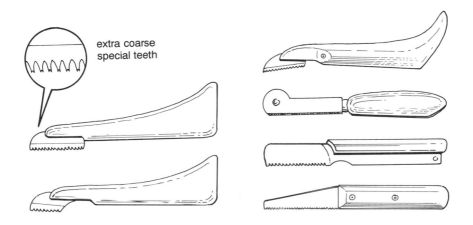

extra coarse
special teeth

Various stripping knives.

Comb One with widely spaced teeth.

Bristle brush A fairly hard bristle brush is very useful for fluffing up the legs without taking precious hair out with it. Also good for keeping dust and dirt out of the body coat and stimulating the skin.

Dolling-up pad A flexible rubber pad with wire pins for brushing up the furnishings.

Rake This is an essential item. It has long serrated teeth, and is used to remove the undercoat.

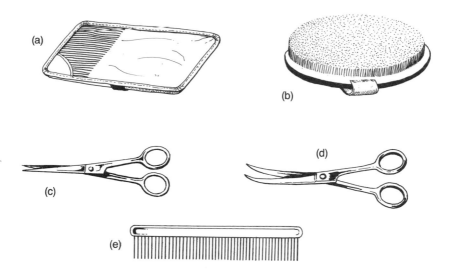

Basic grooming equipment. (a) horsehair glove, useful for polishing;
(b) dolling-up pad; (c) straight scissors; (d) curved scissors;
(e) a comb.

Scissors Curved scissors for cutting the hair between the pads and pointed ones for tidying up the little bits on furnishings that cannot be pulled out.

Another useful aid to producing a well-trimmed dog is a large mirror so that you can see both sides of the dog. Needless to say a room or building with good natural light and electric light is a must.

To grow the tight-fitting hard jacket that the Airedale should be shown in requires quite a lot of hard work. Firstly the long dead coat that the puppy will have grown must be stripped right off. This is done with the stripping knife. The idea is to remove all the long, dead top coat and leave the soft undercoat at this stage. Make sure that the coat is well combed out before making a start. The knife is held between the index finger and thumb. Grip a few hairs between the thumb and the knife and give a sharp tug. Do not grip the hair too far down or undercoat will come out as well. It does help if the skin is held tight with the free hand so that it does not move with every pull. This will also make the process more comfortable for the dog. Always pull the hair in the direction it is growing otherwise holes may appear in the undercoat giving a moth-eaten appearance.

Various stages of trimming. Untrimmed (left), body stripped but furnishings left rough (centre), and the body stripped down close with the furnishings tidied (right).

Start by stripping the body coat. Commence behind the withers along the back to the base of the tail and down the ribs leaving just a little hair on the brisket. Strip the hair off the loins, hips and tail. The most difficult part to trim is the back of the hindquarters, particularly of a male. Great care must be taken to trim off just a few hairs at a time and, as always, pulling the way the hair grows. Trim the hair off inside the hindquarters, on the tummy and take off any long straggly hairs on the insides of the hocks. Return to the back of the head and strip from the occiput bone down the crest of the neck to the body, then each side of the neck and each shoulder down to the front legs. Lift up the head and strip down from the corners of the mouth to the top of the front legs. Strip the hair off the top and sides of the skull, leaving plenty of eyebrow to shape up later. Finally trim the ears very carefully as they are very thin and sensitive and if nicked they will bleed copiously. Once the ears get chaps or sores on them they will take months to heal properly, especially in cold winds or frosty weather.

If the dog has had the dead leg and brisket hair stripped off for some while, the new hair should now be growing through quite well. Comb the legs up and tidy off any straggly bits. The same applies to the brisket hair. Some people like to strip off all the undercoat at this stage but others keep working on the coat until the new hard hair grows through. To help this new hair through brush the coat with the pin pad – carefully – and the bristle brush and comb daily to promote the hard coat. After a few weeks use the rake as well to start removing

97

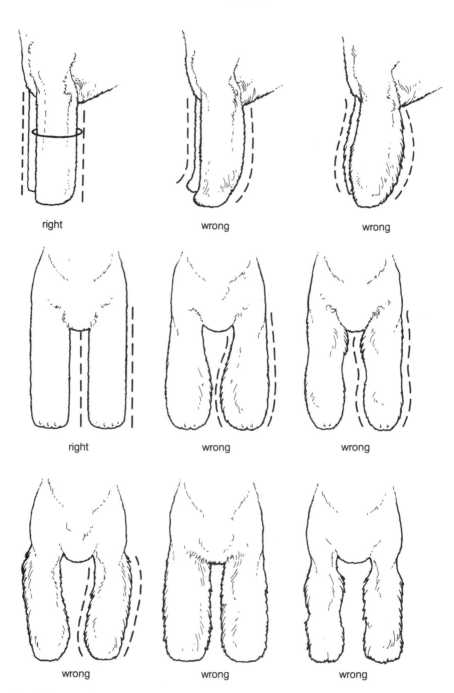

Correct and incorrect leg trims.

the undercoat so that the new coat can come through. The rake will now play as important a part as the trimming knife in the preparation for show. (There are incidentally some stripping knives that make excellent rakes.)

Rake and brush every other day and the new coat will soon come through, first of all along the back and then down the ribs and loin. As the new hard hair grows through (the time this takes varies with each dog), keep the coat tidy by trimming off any straggly or loose hairs. The idea is to grow a tight-fitting, hard jacket that will shine naturally because there is no woolly 'rubbish' in it. It is super to see a dog in really hard condition with the correct healthy coat. Once the coat is through it is not difficult to keep it looking good by continuing the use of rake and brush and by topping. This is as it sounds – just 'top' or trim off the hair that is loose and is spoiling the sharp outline required. Topping must be done very carefully so that hard coat is left, it can be done by finger and thumb or very carefully with a stripping knife.

About two and a half weeks before the show, trim the head, ears, throat, sides of neck, shoulders, behind the tail and back of hind-quarters really close, and tidy up the leg hair and shape the eyebrows and whiskers. Remember that each different length of hair should blend into the next. Get to know the faults of your dog so that you can try to hide these from view by trimming. Of course it will not fool the judge but it will certainly make the dog look better!

Keep working on the whole dog, continually trimming the parts that need to be very short so that there is just a covering of smooth new hair. The skull, ears, shoulders, throat, front and back of tail need to be short and the crest of neck and body should have a longer, hard coat. Rake and brush the neck and body coat and keep the outline of the dog as tidy as possible. It is a good idea to get a picture of a correctly trimmed dog to pin up in the grooming room, so that you can see what you are aiming for.

The shoulder hair should be tapered into the front leg hair by trimming closely on the outside of the elbow and by blending into the leg hair so that there is no hair to flap about when the dog moves. The front legs should look straight when viewed from any angle.

The hair over the hips and top of the thigh muscles should be short but blending in with the longer hair at that point. The hair inside the quarters should be short, as should the hair at the back of the legs to show the bend of stifle. Leave the hair a little longer on the back of the hocks, but keep it very tidy. Comb the leg hair up and tidy it round

99

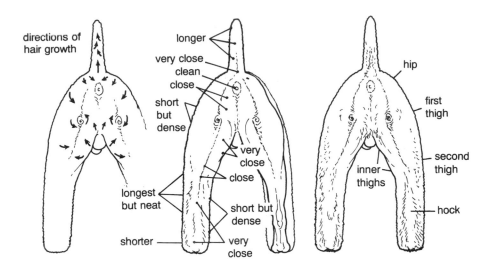

Trimming the hindquarters.

the feet. Trim off all you can with the knife or finger and thumb and finish off with scissors. You should be keeping the hair cut out between the pads and the nails well filed back as a matter of routine but, be sure to give them another going over a few days before the show.

The shaping of the eyebrows and whiskers are probably the most difficult and the most vital to get just right. The expression is such an important part of the Airedale Terrier as it conveys the whole essence and character of the dog. If a lot of hair is left around the eyes they cannot be seen, and much of the expression is in the eyes. Apart from that we do not want our Airedales' expressions to resemble Kerry Blue or Lakelands.

Trim very close on the outside corner of the eye and leave more on the inside corner. The eyebrows should blend into the skull hair and not be too long or too bushy. Trim off virtually hair by hair, continually looking at what you have done to see if it looks all right. Trim the hair very close on the cheeks and down to the corners of the mouth. The hair on the foreface must be shaped as well without too much being taken off. The foreface should look strong and well made up under the eyes but not so full of hair that it looks as though the dog has toothache, nor should too much hair be taken off or the foreface will look weak and snipey. Long straggly hairs should be taken off in front of, and between, the eyes with finger and thumb and

Close-up of the trim of the head. The length of hair can be seen by the length of line.

finished off by scissoring into shape. View the head from all angles to see if any more hair could be taken off to improve or complete the picture. A few days before the show trim the edges of the ears as close as possible and make sure that there is no hair growing out of them.

When you think that you have finished the dog to the best of your abilities, put him on a lead, let him shake and have another look at him. In all probability there will be a few more hairs to be taken off and if someone can move him up and down for you so much the better. You will then be able to see if the legs in particular look all right and there is no hair flapping about that could distort the look of the movement, or maybe a little more could be taken off to make the dog appear to move better. The hair on the belly should be trimmed right off and the brisket hair tidied and tapered into the loin. If your dog is shallow bodied do not be tempted to leave a lot of brisket hair. This only draws attention to the fact.

Once you have the dog in good trim it is fairly easy to keep him in good show coat for quite a long time. Keep going over the coat almost every day with the rake and take off any dead or untidy hair. The

101

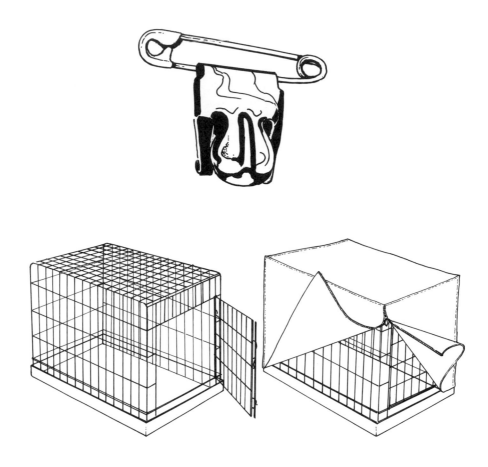

A ring clip (top) and a collapsible cage, with and without cover.

shorter parts, shoulders, head etc, can be gone over every week, thus ensuring the colour will always be bright and fresh. Never be tempted to clip or use a sharp knife or the colour will go dull and dowdy looking. If the leg and whisker hair looks very dirty or greasy, wash them the day before the show with a mild soap or shampoo, rinse thoroughly and dry them into shape. Make sure you tidy them up again afterwards in case they look untidy.

Do not be disappointed if, when you get to the show, your dog does not look as good when compared to most of the others as you hoped he would. Use your eyes and look at the well-presented dogs to see where you should have taken more off or left more on.

102

The finished article.

Most exhibitors are very helpful to newcomers and some of the breed clubs run trimming classes – there may be one near enough for you to go to. Keep practising and watching and you will soon become proficient, but do not expect to win if you are not prepared to put in a lot of work on your dog.

10

Judging

Anybody who wishes to judge at any show must of course have an invitation from the club that is holding the event. The Kennel Club does not have to give its permission for anyone to judge at Limited, Sanction or Open shows. It is for the committee of the club to decide upon who they wish to judge their show and for the club secretary to issue an invitation on their behalf.

Anyone wishing to judge must have been an exhibitor for a number of years and to have proved that they have a good knowledge and understanding of the breed concerned. An important part of being a judge is to be familiar with the procedures in the centre of the ring as well as those outside it. A good way to gain an insight into these procedures is to act as a ring steward for as many experienced and competent judges as possible. One of the Kennel Club's instructions to stewards is that they 'must assist the judge in the course of his/her duties and to ensure the smooth running of the ring'. As a result of this familiarization and observation it should follow that a first-time judge must be more relaxed and therefore be able to concentrate entirely on the judging.

The Kennel Club must give its approval before anyone is given an appointment to judge at a Championship Show where Challenge Certificates are on offer. The proposed judge must have judged the breed at Open shows over a period of at least five years, have judged at least one Breed Club show and have bred or owned winning dogs, preferably some that have won their way into the Kennel Club Stud Book.

The average exhibitor goes to a dog show to get the opinion of the expert on his dog. The majority of dog lovers who show are dedicated to the ultimate perfection of the breed. These exhibitors go to the show to find out how, in the view of the expert, they are progressing towards this end. (There are of course a few less enthusiastic folks who attend dog shows just for a day out to meet their doggy friends!) The exhibitor therefore has the right to assume that the judge possesses a degree of specialist knowledge of the breed. It would be pointless otherwise to show the dog under that particular judge.

Appointing a Judge

In the United Kingdom it seems to be fairly easy to become a judge, but in some countries would-be judges have to undergo quite stringent training and pass examinations before being allowed to judge. In the UK the actual experience of judging at the non-Championship shows takes the place of this. Let us now examine the procedures that must be followed in the UK for a judge to be permitted to award Challenge Certificates in a particular breed. In the UK the ultimate authority is vested in the Kennel Club and the final decision as to the suitability of a particular person to judge at a particular show is made by the General Committee through the judges sub-committee. The breed clubs or, in the case of the Airedale Terrier and certain other breeds, a breed council composed of representatives of all the British Airedale clubs, is invited to consider the suitability of the candidate and offer a detailed opinion which will be taken into account at the Kennel Club. The rules that govern breed councils are explicit and state quite positively that breed councils are consultative bodies without executive powers. Breed councils may make recommendations on the breed standard or, if requested, compile lists of persons who would be supported when judging at different types of shows.

This may be explained more easily by taking a hypothetical example. A judge who has never judged the breed at Championship level is invited by the Midshire Canine Society to judge Airedales and award CCs at their show in two years' time. It is a Kennel Club rule that all judges for Championship shows must be selected at a properly constituted meeting of the show committee. A person who has not previously awarded CCs in the breed that he is nominated to judge, would receive a questionnaire from the show secretary, on which he must detail his experience in judging and winning in the breed. A completed questionnaire must be considered by the show committee and if approved, forwarded to the Kennel Club. The views of the breed council on the prospective judge are then sought and this opinion must be sent to the Kennel Club at least nine months before the show. There is a time limit of six weeks between the receipt of the documents by the breed council, their consideration by the nine British Airedale Terrier Clubs, their return to the breed council for collation and the submission to the Kennel Club. This gives very little time to arrive at a balanced view. Each club sends two delegates to the breed council and between them they have one vote. In the event of a tie in the voting, the chairman of the breed council has the casting vote. The detailed result of the vote, with reasons, is sent to the judges' sub-committee at the Kennel Club who may or may not take notice of the result. We shall assume that the breed council considered the judge to be worthy to award CC's and that the judge's sub-committee also agreed. The judge's appointment would then be announced in the

The late Mollie Harmsworth examining an exhibit at an outdoor show.

Kennel Gazette. No announcement is made until the approval of the Kennel Club General Committee has been obtained.

A Good Judge

There are some points pertaining to judges and judging that must be remembered. It is essential that the exhibitor accepts gracefully the decisions of the judge. By entering under a judge the exhibitor makes an implied acceptance of the judge's placement and decisions: he should not enter under any judge whose rulings he cannot accept.

For most people a dog show is a relaxation or hobby to be enjoyed whether judge or judged and should not be spoiled by unusual or idiosyncratic conduct by the person chosen to judge the dogs (or by exhibitors come to that). It must also be remembered that the placements are the judge's personal interpretations of the Breed Standard. Inevitably, all the other judges at the ringside will have their own opinions, many of which will differ considerably from those of the 'man in the middle'. However, the judge is also being judged and his decisions may be questioned by the spectators at the ringside, but not by the exhibitors.

It is said that in the early days of the Airedale in Yorkshire, any disapproval of the judge's ruling would come very vocally from the ringside and it has been recorded that more than one judge made a very rapid and undignified retreat with spectators in hot pursuit! Another judge at another show on another day may place the dogs quite differently – one reason being that the other judges' ideas will be that different things are important. One judge may consider that movement is all important while another may place greater stress on colour of eye or condition of coat. Each judge is, or should be, judging the dogs on the day.

A judge should try to start on time just as he expects exhibitors to arrive on time. A good judge should have complete command of the ring, be firm in decisions, not take too long to decide on placings, nor change placings once decided upon. He must not allow himself to be intimidated by mutterings or loud comments by any exhibitor in the ring, nor by the glaring or staring of any exhibitor. He must be unbiased and fair, not allow himself to get flustered in the ring and of course have an inside and out knowledge of the breed, with the 'eye' to carry it all out. The perfect judge – there are a few!

Ch. Tanworth Merriment, seen here with his proud owner Mrs Barbara Holland. The judge (far left) has chosen Merriment as his best exhibit. The trophies have been presented and now they are posing for photographs. A job well done by the judge and the end of a perfect day for dog and owner. All concerned are justifiably pleased with their labours.

The most critical judges are the ones sitting round the ring –not only judging the judge but ready to pull the exhibits to pieces as well. This is why you should keep your dog looking as good as possible at all times. There is always the possibility that amongst the ringsiders there is someone due to judge at a forthcoming show; and he will certainly have more time whilst sitting at the ringside to find fault than when he is himself the judge. On the other hand if the ringsiders, who are a very knowledgeable bunch, do express admiration for any dog, you can be sure that it really is a 'good 'un'.

There is no place in dog showing for either arrogance or petulance. As was mentioned earlier, the solution lies with the exhibitor who can show confidence by his entry or lack of confidence by his absence.

Show secretaries would soon get the message and no longer invite judges who draw poor entries. Should any exhibitors so express their distaste by not supporting a particular judge, they must also deny themselves the pleasure of showing their dogs. We must say though that this type of judge is seldom seen and usually dog shows are the happy, friendly affairs that they should be.

When a judge steps into the centre of the ring he will be looking for dogs that come as close to his idea of the perfect Airedale Terrier as possible. He will expect to see the dogs in front of him presented in good trim and able to move properly on a lead. The exception to this rule would be puppies who would probably not be penalized for misbehaving!

He has a right to expect that no exhibitor would bring a dog under him that is vicious or likely to bite (hopefully there are none of those in our breed!). He will be looking for a number of exhibits that conform to the Standard so that he will be able to put dogs of the same type in his final four or five placings in each class. The dog and bitch that in his opinion come closest to the ideal in conformation, character, coat and showmanship will be the winners. If it is an All-Breed show he will want to send into the Terrier Group an Airedale Terrier that displays all the characteristics of the King of Terriers. A dog with soundness, type and that something extra that makes him stand out from the rest. That one in his opinion will be the Best of Breed.

One of the duties of a judge is to write a critique on the first and second placings in each class. The reason for these critiques is that we all like to read what the judge thinks of our dogs, although we do not always agree with his opinions! However, we have paid quite a lot of money, not to mention all the hard work involved in getting the dog ready for the show, so we do like to read about the reasoning behind the decisions. It must be appreciated that writing a critique is fairly hard work and some judges are loath to do it. Most manage to write good ones, and some even write very constructively and with great flair. Occasionally a judge will write glowingly about his own dog's progeny but with a little malice about a rival's dogs even if he has had to place them highly because of merit, but these are few and far between and can be the cause of great amusement. Another judge may delight in writing a damning report on a top-winning dog just for the sake of it and this can be very hard on a good dog if, later, an unsure and inexperienced judge is influenced by the report and puts the dog down because of it.

Occasionally a judge will damn a dog without giving a reason but indicating that there is some part of the dog that is really bad. Here

109

again an inexperienced or weak judge may put this dog down, finding many and varied faults that the poor dog probably does not have.

Overseas readers of these critiques must be puzzled at times to read the variety of opinions from different judges and wonder if they are writing about the same dog. On the whole though judges take the writing of a critique as seriously as they do their judging. In the 'old days' if a particular judge was on the staff of one of the English dog papers he could not send his critique to the other one for publication. In that case the other paper commissioned someone else to write the critique – quite often that someone was an exhibitor at the show, which could hardly encourage true and accurate reporting. Happily this no longer seems to happen. In some countries the judge has to write a report on each dog immediately it has been judged, and a copy of this is given to each exhibitor when judging is finished. In America, Canada and Australia no written report is required.

11

Ailments and Diseases

If a human appears to be ill or out of sorts it is usually comparatively easy to find out what is wrong. The patient can say what the discomfort is and where it is located. A canine patient is very much at a disadvantage in that there can be no actual communication of symptoms although often much can be learnt by his behaviour. It had been thought that most dogs had a higher pain threshold than humans but modern veterinary thinking suggests that animals feel the same level of pain as human beings, but are unable to express it as we can. As a result of recent research, it is felt that we should assume that most animals feel the same degree of pain that we do. Consequently, greater emphasis is now being put on the use of analgesics in the veterinary world for animals in situations where with human beings, their use would be routine. It becomes a matter of deciding on the seriousness of the condition by observing the various signs which may be apparent. As with humans, reaction to pain varies greatly between individual dogs.

Skin irritation can be observed if the dog is forever scratching. Severe worm infestation is generally indicated by loss of weight or loss of appetite and regular administration of worming pills acts as a prophylactic measure. Prevention is, of course, far better than cure and by following a few simple and basic rules a good deal of discomfort and illness can be avoided. The first, and one of the most important, measures is the provision of a regular diet of fresh and nourishing food. We are all, human and canine, better able to resist disease and infection if we are well fed. Just as vital to your dog's health is the provision of clean, dry living quarters with plenty of well-aired clean bedding. There must always be a plentiful supply of fresh drinking water which should be changed frequently. A dog requires plenty of exercise and there is really no substitute for road walking for at least some of the time. Road walking keeps the nails short and keeps the dog up on his toes. When there is too much exercising on grass, the dog's nails do not get worn and must, therefore be cut. However, dogs do not like to have their nails cut, and so it is far easier the other way. To return to the question of exercise: on a cold wet day in winter, you may not want to leave the fireside and miss the TV but your dog does – he is a creature of habit and it is essential that he has his exercise – it probably will not do you much harm either. Airedales do not seem to be prone to many of the conditions suffered by some other breeds. Although 'man-made', Airedales do not exhibit any of the exaggerations which plague some of the 'fancy' breeds.

Any unexpected change in appearance or behaviour of your dog must immediately alert you to the possibility that something may be amiss. Having come to the conclusion that all is not well, a further decision must be made as to the seriousness of the condition. Should professional advice be sought? Can the condition be dealt with at home? Will it get better without treatment? Is masterly inactivity the best solution? These thoughts will pass through your mind and you must consider all the facts at your disposal. If there is any doubt at all in your mind, give your veterinary surgeon a ring and be on the safe side. Signs that something is wrong can usually be seen if one is alert. There are a number of indications that can be warnings of trouble in store and these should always be borne in mind.

Symptoms of Ill Health

Unexpected coughing.
Loss of appetite, extending for more than 48 hours may cause concern.
Diarrhoea and vomiting.
Constipation? Unusual colour of stools. Blood in faeces.
Rubbing the ears, eyes or mouth may indicate pain.
Anal pain, manifested by rubbing affected area.
Scratching.
Sleeping more than usual.
Loss of weight. Eating well but still losing weight.
Dog is lack lustre. No interest in normal activities and pastimes.
Limping and favouring one leg.
Pain when touched.
Obvious pain when walking can indicate one or more of a number of ailments.
Loss of energy – tired by exercise (i.e. reduced exercise tolerance).

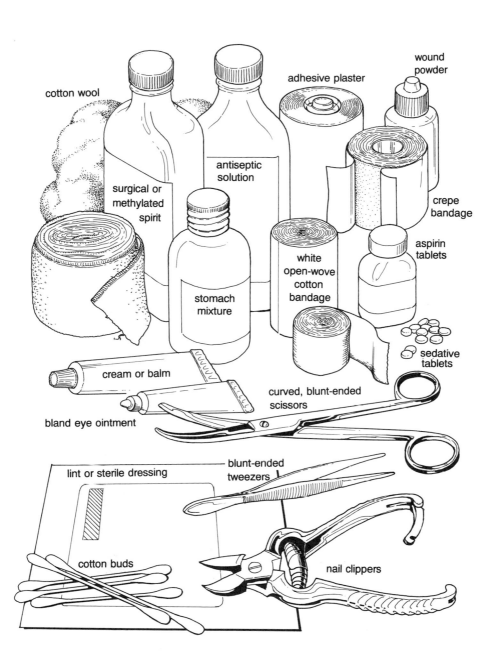

A dog's first-aid kit

Excessive drinking. In hot weather or after prolonged exercise, it is not unexpected or unusual for a dog to drink more than normal. Try to gauge objectively how much the dog is actually drinking. One can get a false impression of the amount a dog has actually drunk. A bitch feeding her puppies naturally requires a greater fluid intake. If the dog does not fall into these categories and continues to drink more than normal, call for advice.

We will now deal with some of the conditions that may affect your dog. Many of these are avoidable if the correct preventive measures are followed.

Parasites

The term parasite may be defined as an animal or plant living in or upon another and drawing nutriment directly from it. There are many parasites that can infest and live off your dog if proper care and precautions have been neglected. Parasites can be divided into internal (endoparasites) and external (ectoparasites) and the treatment differs for the two types. Internal parasites in the main comprise worms of various kinds and the treatment generally is prophylactic and consists of a rigidly adhered-to worming programme.

Endoparasites

The commonest types of endoparasites that will be encountered are:

Hookworm Hookworm (*Uncinaraia Stenocephala*) is the northern or cold climate hookworm. The small, round worms of $3/4$in (2cm) in length live in the small intestine. Transmission of this hookworm is facilitated when a number of dogs use the same grass exercising runs.

Whipworm Whipworm (*Trichuris Vulpis*) also occurs in larger kennels where numbers of dogs use the same grass areas. The whipworm grows to 3in (7cm) in length and is found in the caecum.

Lungworm Lungworm (*Filaroides Osleri*) is found in nodules in the trachea and bronchii and is the third parasite often found in larger kennels. This parasite poses some difficulties in diagnosis and treatment. Some cases are symptomless but others cause a dry racking cough.

114

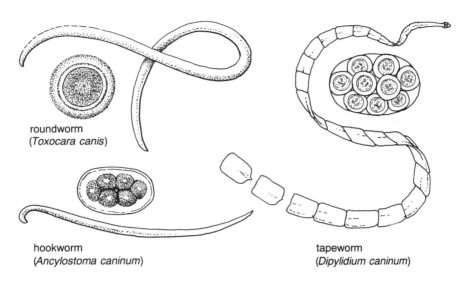

roundworm
(*Toxocara canis*)

hookworm
(*Ancylostoma caninum*)

tapeworm
(*Dipylidium caninum*)

Dog worms with eggs.

Tapeworm Tapeworm (*Dipylidium caninum*) infests the small intestine of dogs. It grows up to 20in (50cm) in length and its life cycle includes fleas and many other animals as intermediate hosts.

Roundworm Roundworm (*Toxicara canis*) and its control are of the greatest importance because humans, especially children, are particularly at risk. The worm measures up to 6in (15cm) in length and as the name suggests, it is round and white. The minute eggs can be ingested by children or other dogs from the ground, from the fur or from the bedding of an infected animal.

Heartworm This parasite is not often seen in the United Kingdom, but is endemic in tropical or subtropical areas of Asia, Australia, Central America and parts of the USA where mosquitoes transmit the larval form of the worm. Treatment is by means of a daily prophylactic tablet but it is reported that the introduction of a new drug has reduced the timescale to one tablet each month. If an imported dog is found to be infected, successful treatment can sometimes be carried out in two or three days.

To prevent endoparasitic infestation we can only re-emphasize the importance of a regular worming programme which must be strictly adhered to throughout the lifetime of the dog. If there is any suspicion that your dog has been infected with worms, obtain a sample of the dog's faeces and take the sample to your vet who will be able to identify the parasite and advise on the appropriate treatment.

Ectoparasites

Because of the close relationship between man and dog it is inevitable that some of the canine parasites include man somewhere in their life cycle.

Ectoparasites are parasites living outside the body, on the body or in the skin. The most frequent and easily discernible sign is pruritus or persistent severe itching. Scratching temporarily relieves the itching by substituting overriding pain sensations but skin damage can result. It is more desirable to remove the cause if possible. In a dog, as in a human, boredom and inactivity can favour the itch-scratch syndrome.

The main ectoparasites met with in our canines are listed below:

Mange Sarcoptic Mange (Scabies) is caused by the parasitic mite *Sarcoptes scabei canis*. It burrows into the epidermis and the female lays her eggs there. Itching is intense but does not develop until sometime after infestation is established and so the signs could be taken as those of some other condition. This condition is almost impossible to treat successfully without help from your veterinary surgeon. There may be considerable irritation of head, ears and elbows from the continued scratching. The mites can be killed fairly easily by your veterinary surgeon but re-infection is always possible if precautions are not taken. Demodectic mange, caused by a different mite, does not cause as much irritation but is very difficult to get rid of and veterinary advice must be sought. It usually starts with a single bare patch which looks dirty greyish in colour.

Fleas Fleas cause pruritus by simple mechanical irritation – crawling on the skin: bites can also be irritating. Clinically flea allergy dermatitis is also known as summer eczema and is accompanied by severe itching and an exudative dermatitis which can be aggravated by the efforts of the dog to relieve the condition. Treatment and prevention of flea infestations can be long and drawn out – cats sometimes provide a ready supply of fleas for re-infestation and must also receive attention. Flea collars and medication are rarely enough without other

116

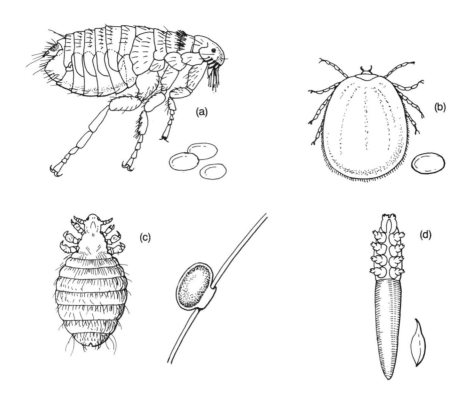

External parasites: (a) dog flea, (b) dog tick, (c) dog louse,
(d) demodectic mange mite.

treatment. An effective method of combating flea infestation is bathing the dog every week or so for about a month. The bath should contain an insecticidal agent that will kill the fleas. The dead fleas can then be groomed out with a fine toothcomb. It is essential that all bedding and places where the dog has been should be thoroughly treated to prevent any recurrence.

Lice Lice can also be a problem, particularly in groups of puppies (breeding kennels or pet shops). Infestation is usually around the head and neck, and causes severe itching. Bathing in insecticidal shampoo is usually effective.

Ticks Ticks in larval forms may cause itching in dogs.

Harvest Mites These mites can be found in straw, hay, grain and carpets, and occur most frequently in the summer and autumn. The straw itch mite occupies hay, grain and straw and will cause itching in both dogs and humans. Generally veterinary advice should be sought if the cause is not obvious and the cure not sure and simple.

Ear Mites Ear mites cannot be seen by the naked eye but will cause severe irritation in the ear and requires immediate treatment as it can very easily be transmitted from one animal to another.

Infectious Diseases

There are a number of conditions where prophylactic inoculation is necessary to control the infection and prevent the onset of the disease. It is essential that this programme of inoculation be discussed with your veterinary advisor at an early stage.

Canine Distemper

Canine Distemper is generally to be found in young unvaccinated dogs of any breed, usually younger than a year old and the peak period is 3–6 months. Onset of the condition can happen quite rapidly and is often preceded by coughing, vomiting, diarrhoea and signs of fever, but if a dog has been regularly vaccinated, he is very unlikely to get distemper. There is no specific cure. Broad spectrum antibiotics help to control secondary infection but have no effect on the causal virus itself. As the condition is generally to be found in very young dogs, it is essential that the puppy is vaccinated at an early age. The presence of maternal antibodies controls the condition until the puppy may be safely vaccinated without fear of neutralization. One of the signs of canine distemper is a thickening of the pads which gave it the name 'Hard Pad', but this is not a commonly seen symptom. Ask your veterinary surgeon to call rather than risk taking a highly infectious puppy to the surgery.

Leptospirosis

Leptospirosis comes in two forms, one of which generally affects the kidneys, and the other the liver. There may be an overlap and one bacterium has an association with the other condition. Preventive inoculation has drastically reduced the incidence of infection by these bacteria.

Leptospira canicola This causes a disease which occurs mainly in urban areas and affects the kidneys. Luckily most dogs suffer only a relatively mild infection. If the condition is severe, it can result in kidney failure. Both strains of Leptospirosis can affect man. Administration of antibiotics by your veterinary surgeon can clean up the infection. Prevention is better than cure.

Leptospina icterohaemorrhagiae This is a bacterium carried by rats and the disease can be transferred to dogs and also to humans when it is called Weils disease. It is thus important to exercise care if contact is made with an infected dog. It is also noteworthy that the dog will pass the bacteria in his urine during the infection and for months afterwards. Disinfection is not easy and inoculation is the answer.

Canine Parvovirus

The method of infection is generally by mouth and because the virus is very resistant to destruction, large amounts of infected faeces are deposited into the environment. The condition can affect a dog at any age but it is most frequent in puppies. The signs that are most common in the dogs are severe vomiting and later diarrhoea, weight loss and dehydration. If the dog is to survive, fluid replacement therapy is essential as well as thorough disinfection of the premises and the dog runs. Parvovirus is resistant to most disinfectants. Formaldehyde and bleach are effective for a short time only as they are made non-effective by organic material. There are, however, very effective parvocidal disinfectants available.

Parainfluenza (Kennel Cough)

This condition is caused by a virus which some authorities think might be responsible for some outbreaks of kennel cough-like diseases. Bordatella is the organism that probably causes most outbreaks of kennel cough. A nasal vaccine is used against this condition. Droplet infection is contracted by inhaling infected air and is generally transmitted from one dog to another. The most obvious sign is a sharp cough and adult dogs may continue to eat and behave normally but

119

with puppies the condition can be more serious. A vaccine which is pushed up the nasal passages by a syringe forms the basis of preventive treatment. It is probably wise to have a prophylactic inoculation before putting your Airedale into a boarding kennels. Kennel cough is highly infectious.

Infectious Canine Hepatitis

Infectious Canine Hepatitis is caused by a virus which can be excreted from an infected animal in saliva, faeces or urine. Thus all these are possible sources of infection. Infected urine should not be discounted as a vehicle for the transmission of the virus. The virus can be excreted in the urine for more than six months after the dog's recovery. It seems that actual dog to dog contact or contact with infected material is essential for infection to occur. Measures to isolate puppies reduce the likelihood of the disease. Puppies in their first year are the most susceptible. Signs include loss of appetite, vomiting and diarrhoea while a jaundice may be seen in the eyes. Some dogs (20 per cent) recovering from the disease show a corneal oedema (blue eye).

Rabies

Rabies is a fatal condition caused by a virus which attacks the central nervous system. There are various signs of the disease in dogs but basically it may be divided into 'dumb' or 'furious' rabies. To a large extent these descriptions are self- explanatory. Furious Rabies is comparatively easy to spot – a normally placid dog becomes ferocious. The dumb form is harder to see – the dog is affected by a nerve paralysis, and a normally aloof dog becomes dependent and affectionate. This, though harder to diagnose, is the more common form.

The disease is endemic in many countries. Antarctica and Australia are the only continents free of the condition, although in Europe some countries are still not affected by the disease. Among the unaffected countries are Britain and Ireland. In continental Europe the disease is endemic and only strictly adhered-to quarantine laws have prevented large scale infection in this country. Following infection by a bite, the saliva of the affected dog carries the virus. The dog seldom lives more than five days from the clinical onset of the disease. Once the brain is infected it proceeds down the cranial nerves and there is no cure. A human bitten by a rabid dog always dies.

Modern vaccines give a high degree of protection and all dogs exported to areas where rabies is endemic must have rabies vaccine inoculation.

Hip Dysplasia

This subject has come into prominence during the last few years. There is a malfunction in either one or both hip joints and the condition can be very painful to the dog. Generally, it is associated with the larger breeds and is thought to be, at least to some extent, hereditary. In many countries severe restrictions are placed on breeding from dogs who are affected. In the UK a scheme run jointly by the Kennel Club and the British Veterinary Association evaluates the severity of the condition using radiography. There is a panel of very experienced veterinary surgeons who produce a 'hip score'. It is essential that Airedale owners, particularly those who intend to have a litter or to allow their dog to be used at stud, should have the dogs hip scored. Put yourself in the hands of your veterinary surgeon. He will advise about procedure.

Other Complaints

It is of course not always necessary to consult the veterinary surgeons who are usually very busy people and will not appreciate being called out to your dog unnecessarily. If your dog seems to be off colour or to be in pain it is essential not to panic. The situation should be appraised quickly and methodically. Decide whether the condition is serious enough to warrant a surgery visit or a house call from the vet or whether it is something that can be dealt with at home by a simple remedy or even by masterly inactivity, allowing nature to effect a cure.

Vomiting and Diarrhoea

If your dog only vomits on one occasion, he is probably reacting in nature's way to get rid of something that should not have been ingested in the first place or because the stomach is temporarily out of order. The best treatment is certainly to leave well alone but if the vomiting and diarrhoea continue and there is blood in the motions all food should be withheld and the dog kept warm. If the dog is weak and in a state of collapse, take him at once to the surgery, otherwise go to the next normal surgery. Should there be no blood in the stools but there is looseness the first step is a diet change: take the dog off meat and milk and give him cooked fish or chicken with rice instead of biscuit. Call the vet if the condition does not improve. It is necessary to use common sense before deciding on any home treatment.

In order to prevent travel sickness your dog should be taken for short rides at first and then the distance gradually built up. If your dog tends to travel sickness then it is advisable not to feed large meals just before a journey.

Constipation

Constipation is another condition that may affect your dog and could be the result of any of a number of causes. These are mainly dietary e.g. too much protein and insufficient roughage. The best prophylactic treatment is correct feeding, providing clean water at all times and clean dry bedding in the sleeping quarters. A good nutritional diet is of the greatest importance in maintaining the health of your dog. The Airedale is a large outdoor dog and therefore plenty of exercise is vital to his well-being. If you are not prepared to give plenty of exercise, then you should buy yourself a small lap dog, not an Airedale Terrier.

Skin Conditions and Cysts

Rough-coated terriers are very prone to skin conditions and one of the commonest causes is incorrect diet. To begin with, keep the coat short and well-combed, at the same time making certain that your dog is receiving an adequate balanced diet. It takes just one flea bite to cause severe itching which your dog will try to relieve by scratching. By this time the flea has probably departed for pastures new, and the dog has chewed a hole in his coat and often through the skin. This often occurs near the tail or on the hip. A few drops of Evening Primrose Oil daily on his food will work wonders in getting the hair back. Dandruff is another condition that may affect your Airedale and it can be treated by a lotion of Benzyl Benzoate or by special shampoos.

Eczema, wet or dry, is a fairly common skin condition and treatments can be effected with special shampoos or lotions such as Benzyl Benzoate. If the coat is stripped or clipped off it is easier to get down to the problem areas.

Interdigital cysts are another condition which can be very painful.

Soaking in warm salt water can help but sometimes lancing is necessary. The dog will usually be very lame. Strained muscles and torn ligaments cause pain and limping. If there is no improvement in a couple of days, seek professional help.

Bites and Stings

Dogs are inquisitive creatures and sometimes have a too-close look at wasps and bees: should your Airedale be stung by a bee he will experience considerable pain. Try to locate the sting and pull it out. Wasps do not leave their stings behind but the area of the sting or where the bee sting was removed should be bathed with bicarbonate of soda. If this is not easily available put on an old-fashioned 'blue bag' or rub with a raw onion. If the sting is in the mouth the area should be swabbed frequently with surgical spirit; if this is not to hand whisky or methylated spirit will do.

If your dog is bitten by a snake, veterinary attention should be sought straight away. In the meantime do not allow the dog to move and try to bandage above the bite between it and the heart before going to the surgery. If your dog has a fight and is bitten keep the wound clean but do not allow it to heal too quickly or an abcess may form.

Anal Glands

Sometimes the anal glands which are just under the skin and slightly below and on each side of the anus become blocked or impacted and

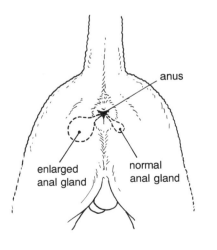

The anal glands.

anus

enlarged
anal gland

normal
anal gland

should be emptied. They are not emptying naturally if the dog is dragging its bottom along the ground. The vet will empty the glands but once shown you should be able to do it yourself. The fluid is rather smelly – it should be excreted when the dog passes a motion to mark his territory.

Ears, Eyes and Teeth

Airedale Terriers are a dropped ear breed and thus are prone to problems in this region unless precautions are taken to ensure that the hair within the ears is removed to allow them to be kept clean. It is very important that the temptation to poke into the ears with anything hard is resisted. A close check should also be kept on the mouth in order to ensure that nothing wedges between the teeth. These should be clean and devoid of tartar. Dogs love marrow bones which not only keep them amused for hours but provide essential nutrition. As a bonus they keep the teeth clean and tartar free. Eyes are also an area where care must be exercised in order to keep the dog healthy. Most conditions of the eye require expert help but bland eye lotions or a small blob of eye cream in the corner of the eye can be used safely when the eyes are inflamed and watering.

Heat stroke is another common occurrence which is often the result of a careless owner failing to provide sufficient ventilation for dogs left in cars. Should this happen any treatment must be quick to be effective. The body temperature has to be lowered by ice packs or sponges of cold water and ten minutes should be enough to bring the temperature down. If recovery is not fast, seek veterinary attention.

Dogs can easily suffer from shock as the result of an accident or because of burns or scalds. Fright and severe pain can also cause shock. The treatment is to keep the dog warm with blankets and hot water bottles if necessary.

12

Famous Dogs of the Breed

A chapter like this must begin somewhere and where better than immediately after the acceptance of the breed by the Kennel Club. There is the story of Thunder, an ordinary Airedale, who though not a fighting dog was pitted against a trained Bull Terrier and who, after a cruel battle, killed his opponent. The early black and tan Terriers were too light for the fighting pit. The fact that their temperament was not suited to dog fighting made Thunder's achievement more noteworthy.

Airedale Terrier Thunder who was matched against a fighting Bull Terrier and emerged the victor. This seems to be his main claim to fame. Note the collar!

Another dog who made an impressive contribution to the breed was Airedale Jerry. Jerry was never a champion but he sired a large number of great offspring among whom was Ch. Cholmondeley Briar, cited by Holland Buckley as one of the soundest dogs in his memory. Master Briar, a grandson of Ch. Cholmondeley Briar also exercised considerable influence on the quality of the breed by siring many champions including Ch. Clonmel Monarch, Ch. Tone Masterpiece, Ch. Mistress Royal and Ch. Rock Salt. In his turn Ch. Clonmel Monarch also appears to have been a remarkably successful stud dog, being the sire of many top quality Airedale Terriers among whom were Ch. Broadlands Royal Descendant, Ch. Tone Regent and Ch. Clonmel Bedrock.

Airedale Terriers were recognized as a definite breed at the Kennel Club in November 1885 and the first Airedale Champion, Newbold Test, was made up in 1891 to be followed in the same year by Rustic Lad, Wharfedale Rush and the first Airedale bitch Champion, Vixen III. According to Holland Buckley he and his partner Royston Mills received an imperative summons to 'come to Surbiton and buy the best Airedale alive'. The deal was struck and Warfield Victor was renamed Clonmel Marvel and he was made up in 1897. Between the end of the century and the start of the First World War there were a further seven Clonmel champions.

Other kennels of note at this time were Mr Elder's Tone Kennel at Taunton in Somerset which produced five champions, Mr Jennings' Dumbartons who had four more champions to join Dumbarton Lass who was made up in 1897. Among a number of other kennels which were active and successful during this period were the Masters from Cheltenham, the Cromptons of the Leaver Brothers and Clarksons' Broadlands Kennel. There were of course many others worthy of mention if space permitted to record them all. This period saw a significant change in the make and shape of the Airedale. At the end of the century the dogs were longer in the back, heads were coarser, tails were shorter and furnishings much sparser. Thus after the First World War we can see a shortening of the back, an increase of furnishings and a much more pronounced black saddle.

Only a few of the pre-war kennels were still active three years later when dog shows began again in earnest after the end of the war. The Wrose Kennel of Hildebrand Wilson and the Clonmels were joined by a number of new affixes on the post-war scene. Of all the dogs whose contributions to the breed were exceptional, the name of Walnut King Nobbler stands out. Although not a champion himself, the dog sired

Ch. Barton of Burdale – winner of Best in Show at National Terrier Show 1950 beating 820 Terriers, the first time that a novice dog and novice owner had won this award. Miss Jones went on to make up many champions and Airedales were her great love right up to her death in 1990.

twelve champions and his name is to be found in the extended pedigrees of many of today's top dogs. Walnut King Nobbler's sire was the famous Ch. Clee Courtier, himself a very prepotent stud dog whose sire was Clonmel Monarque. Clonmel Monarque sired twelve champions in all. A.J. 'Towyn' Edwards owned a dog called Ch. Mespot Tinker who was sire to a number of champions in the years between the wars.

Influencing the Breed

At this time there were a number of kennels that exerted considerable influence on the development of the Airedale Terrier. J.P. Hall's Warland Kennels had Warland Enchantress as foundation bitch. She was mated to Ch. Rhosddu Royalist and produced Ch. Warland Strategy who was mated to Tom Trees Cragsman Dictator. This alliance resulted in one of the outstanding Airedales of all time – Ch. Warland Ditto – who in turn sired Ch. Warland Whatnot. The Warland Kennel under J.P. Hall and his daughter continued to produce quality dogs: there were fourteen champions during the inter war period. Ch. Warland Protector had a very successful show career in the United Kingdom before being sent to the United States where he was mated to Ch. Covert Dazzle. This mating produced a really outstanding Airedale Terrier named Shelterock Merry Sovereign who became an American Champion and then was brought to the UK in 1937. Ch.

Ch. Shelterock Merry Sovereign. This dog was bred in America by S.M. Stewart from a dog and bitch he bought in England. His sire Ch. Warland Protector was runner up, or Reserve Best in Show at Crufts. Merry Sovereign had such a wonderful career in America that his owner decided to send him to England where he took all before him, including Best in Show at The Kennel Club Show at Olympia – the first Airedale Terrier to win that Cup.

Shelterock Merry Sovereign was Best in Show at the Kennel Club show at Olympia in that year and went on to win twelve Challenge Certificates before returning to the United States. The Warland Kennel was working closely with the Wrose Kennel of Hildebrand Wilson and it can be seen that champions from the one kennel were mated with top dogs from the other. Ch. Wrose Anchor was the sire of four Warland champions.

There were were many other influential kennels at this time: the Tom Trees Cragsman affix appears in the pedigrees of successful dogs and the Towyns, the Llanipsas, the Aislabys, and the Wolstantons all left their mark on the breed. One of the offspring of Walnut King Nobbler that earned the right of recognition was Ch. Aislaby Aethling, winner of thirteen CCs and Terrier Group Winner at Crufts in 1935, and a son of Aethling Champion Aislaby Aethelstan carried on the successful tradition of line breeding practised by this kennel.

Time was already taking its toll and the names of the kennels were changing as new breeders replaced those older men and women. In 1945 the end of hostilities did not bring an immediate resumption of Championship dog shows. However, just ten months after the end of the war the North of England Airedale Terrier Club ran the first Championship Show at the Armoury in Stockport with Mr Cookson as judge. This show was followed in the same year by the National Airedale Terrier Association Show in London, the Midland Counties A.T.C. in Birmingham and, at Stockport again, the North of England

A.T.C. The first post-war Champion was Foxdenton Top Score owned by Miss Hilton who won three of the four Bitch Challenge Certificates at these shows. Brineland Bonnie Boy had two of the dog CCs the others being won by Rural Wyrewood Apollo and Holmbury Bandit. By 1947 showing had returned almost to normal and the names of the breeders and their kennels were becoming more and more familiar. The names of the 1947 Champions were Major Wright's Holmbury Bandit, Anna Care's Rural Wyrewood Apollo, Nan Haslam's Raimon Rhapsody, Mrs Hayes' Aislaby Elzivia, Mr Watson's Brineland Barrier and Mr Kerr's Murraysgate Minstrel.

When Mollie Harmsworth was in partnership with Barbara Roberts they owned a dog called Bengal Lancer who won two CCs before the war but did not secure a third to make a champion. However his claim to fame lies in the delightful story of his fall into a Liverpool canal. Unlike most Airedales Lancer was unable to swim and Mollie had to plunge into the none-too-clean water to haul him out!

The first post-war Crufts was held in 1948 and Jean Hopwood's Ch. Berrycroft Bedlam Bruce was the best Airedale Terrier. Ch. Westhay Fiona was born in 1954 and bred by Irene Hayes, shown by Nan

English and American Ch. Westhay Fiona of Harham, another great bitch to leave these shores and by far the biggest winner of Groups and Best in Shows in the history of the breed in America up to that time (1956–1957).

American Ch. Bengal Sabu – purchased as an unshown yearling by Barbara Strebeigh and Tuck Dell for his pedigree, conformation, type and movement, to breed to their own Airedale Terrier bitches, rather than as a showdog. Sabu did in fact have a fantastic show career! In 1960 and 1961 he was Best of Breed 103 times, had seventy-seven group placings and was seven times Best in Show All Breeds. Barbara Strebeigh says that 'almost every breeding line from England now in America shows a line of descent from Sabu!

Haslam and owned in partnership by the two ladies and she was one of the really outstanding Airedale bitches of all time. Starting at Crufts in 1956 Fiona was awarded the bitch 'ticket' at five successive shows before being sent to the United States. In America Fiona had an even more formidable record of success. Shown on eighty-two occasions Fiona won eighty Best of Breeds, two Best Opposite Sex, sixty Terrier Groups, and twenty-four Best in Shows.

Among other great names that have been sent to America mention should be made of Bengal Sabu, who was unshown in this country and exported in 1959 at one year of age; Sabu took America by storm. Winning Top Airedale Terrier for three years in a row with a total of 103 Best of Breeds out of 108 shows, he also sired a large number of winners that have had a great influence on the breed in the United States. Before leaving this country Sabu sired Bengal Bladud who in turn sired Ch. Bengal Krescent Brave, who in his turn was sire of the famous 'F' litter which included Ch. Jokyl Bengal Figaro – the only true International Champion Airedale.

Figaro was made a Champion in England, sold to Walt Disney to appear in the film *The Ballad of Hector*, was sent to Germany to be campaigned there, and all over the continent, winning many Championships. He went back to America and was made a champion there and in Canada. He then returned to England to win more CCs. Figaro also sired, amongst others, Ch. Jokyl Spaceleader and Ch. Jokyl Queen

Ch. Bengal Krescent Brave. Bred by Tom and Dorothy Hodgkinson whose 'Krescents' were among the very top kennels of the fifties, sixties and early seventies. Krescent Brave was the sire of that famous 'F' litter and many others. His sister Bengal Krescent Ballerina also became a champion and is the maternal grandmother of Ch. Bengal Springtime who is in turn the dam of Ch. Bengal Flamboyant. It is small wonder that this family has produced such a marvellous number of winners.

Ch. Jokyl Spaceleader (1962–1975) – a true Terrier. Great show dog, friend and guardian. A dog with a great sense of humour. 'Jack' was the sire of the great Ch. Jokyl Superman amongst many, and his sire was the star of the Walt Disney film The Ballad of Hector, *Ch. Jokyl Bengal Figaro.*

of Space. Spaceleader then sired Ch. Jokyl Superman who was exported to America after a very successful show career in the UK. His successes in America were quite outstanding. Before he left England he was mated to his aunt Ch. Jokyl Queen of Space to produce American Ch. Jokyl Supermaster, who was sold to America before gaining his English title.

A bitch who never became a champion but made a great contribution to the breed was Bengal Chippinghey Fircone, dam of the aforementioned 'F' litter, Ch. Bengal Gunga Din and Ch. Bengal Lionheart. Incidentally it is interesting to note that Fircone is a

English and American Ch. Jokyl Superman. Many top winning and producing American-breds descend from this dog who led the breed in the States in 1979 and 1980. He was made a champion very quickly in England and Rudi Tegeler put him up at the same show that Bengal Springtime won at. He wrote 'he is a wonderfully balanced dog, excellent in head, eyes and ears, long neck and well-placed shoulders, short well-ribbed body, perfect set on and best of coat and colour. Grand showman, presented in top condition, can only be better in the future'. The latter remark proved to be true as his career in America bore out. 'Tom' is seen here with handler William Thompson winning the coveted Airedale Bowl.

daughter of Olive and George Jackson's (Jokyl) first Airedale Terrier Champion, Mayjack Briar.

Another great Terrier to leave these shores was Ch. Bengal Spring-time, the dam of Ch. Bengal Flamboyant who is the name behind most of the top winners of today. The line runs through his sons Ch. Siccawei Galliard and Ch. Jokyl Smart Guy. A study of pedigrees will reveal that Mollie Harmsworth bred some really beautiful bitches, who

133

Ch. Mayjack Briar was the first dog to be shown by Jokyl Airedales. Bred by George Jackson's daughter Mary, he lived as Olive and George's beloved companion and was the sire of Bengal Chippinghey Fircone who produced the famous 'F' litter (English Champions Jokyl Bengal Figaro and Bengal Fastnet) and American Champions Bengal Frigga and Flyer) and later, English Champions Bengal Gungadin and Jokyl Bengal Lionheart.

were all descended from Krescent Model Maid, another great producer from the famous kennel of Tom and Dorothy Hodgkinson.

So many good Airedale Terriers have left these shores for the United States and other overseas countries that it is really surprising that we can still produce anything of quality. Most of the top kennels – Bengal,

Swedish and English Ch. Bengal Brulyn Sahib bred in the West Country by Millie Bishop, purchased by Mollie Harmsworth, campaigned in England then sold to Sweden. Before he left England, this dog sired Ch. Bengal Springtime.

135

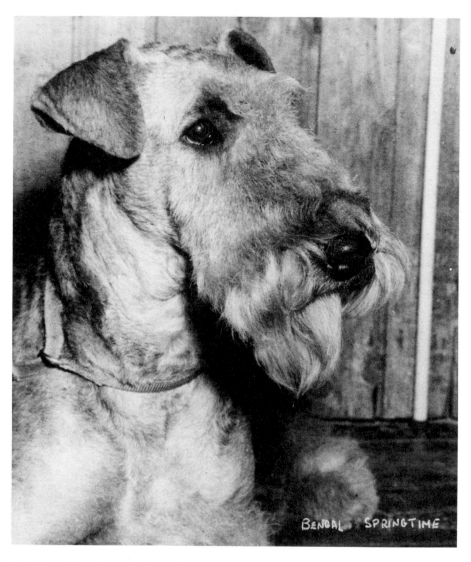

English and American Ch. Bengal Springtime – shown at twenty Championship shows and winning seventeen CCs fourteen with Best of Breed. German breeder/judge Mr Rudi Tegeler wrote of her 'perfect Airedale long lean head, best eyes and ears, wonderful neck and shoulders, excellent ribbed short body, best hindquarters and excellent movement; much substance and absolutely feminine'. Hardly surprising that her son Ch. Bengal Flamboyant has been such an influence on the breed. After the death of Mollie Harmsworth the affix Bengal was passed to David Ashover.

136

Ch. Jokyl Smart Guy – Ch. Bengal Flamboyant's biggest winning
son with twenty CCs to his credit and a different type to Galliard.
Smart Guy had the most beautiful head and eye which is still
coming down through his descendants. Not used much at stud Guy
nevertheless sired a few champions including 1976's Top Dog Ch.
Tanworth Merriment and Top Bitch Ch. Jokyl Smartie Pants.

Tintara Krescent, Burdale, Jokyl and Loudwell in particular – have sent
top stock to many countries over the years.

One dog who did not leave Britain and lived to the age of fourteen
and a half years as the beloved companion of one of his co-owners,
'Mac' Schuth, was Ch. Riverina Tweedsbairn (Ricky), top dog of all

'My impression of Biggles' – an Airedale in an Airedale.

breeds in 1960 and 1961 and Best in Show at Crufts in 1961, a record still unbeaten. He is the only dog to have a party in his honour every year – the Tweedsbairn Party is a well attended affair hosted by the South of England Airedale Terrier Club the weekend after Crufts. Tweedsbairn also officially launched an executive/training aircraft from the Beagle Group – named Airedale.

Tweedsbairn was a combination of the Riverina and Siccawei lines – top winning kennels of their time, along with Krescent, Burdale, Bengal, Jokyl and Tycroit Kennels. Of these, Miss Jones of Burdale fame was the only lady who always showed her own dogs, making history by being the first amateur to make an Airedale dog a champion for sixteen years. She also won Best in Show at The National Terrier Show in 1950 with her first home-bred champion, Ch. Barton of Burdale. Other famous dams are Ch. Siccawei Ruby, willed to Ernest Sharpe by Mrs Clare Halford, and who produced four English champions to Ch. Siccawei Galliard and one to Turith Adonis

Ch. Siccawei Galliard – Ch. Bengal Flamboyant's most famous son and a dog who really caught the eye of the breeders of that time. Galliard was purchased from the estate of Clare Halford by Jokyl Kennels after her death in 1974 and was left in the care of handler Ernest Sharpe who was campaigning him at the time. He won ten CCs and was used at stud by most breeders. He was a very short-backed dog with a very long neck and possessed a really hard black and tan jacket. His stud record proves how right these breeders were, as he has sired seventeen English champions. Strange how fate works, as at the time of her death Mrs Halford was negotiating to sell 'Glen' overseas!

(Galliard's son). This one, Drakehall Debra of Junaken has produced five English champions to Ch. Jokyl Gallipants. Another of the Siccawei Ruby offspring, English Ch. Drakehall Dinah had the distinction of being Best in Show at the Centenary Show in 1976 over a record entry of one hundred and forty-four dogs.

After Tweedsbairn there were many good dogs from a variety of kennels: Loudwell, Mynair, Krescent, Burdale, Bengal, Tintara, Reptonia, Siccawei and Jokyl to name a few. In 1964 a very consistent winner was Margarite of Burdale, owned by George Dale. Ch. Optimist of Mynair was another famous dog of that era, being Best Terrier and runner-up to the Dog of the Year in 1970 before being exported to the United States.

Ch. Tanworth Merriment and Ch. Perrancourt Playful were undoubtedly the outstanding dogs of the seventies. Ch. Tanworth Merriment broke the existing record for the number of Challenge Certificates won by an Airedale Terrier dog, previously held by the 1961 Crufts Best in Show Riverina Tweedsbairn. Ch. Jokyl Smartie Pants had the bitch record of eighteen CCs. This record lasted only a short time before Ch. Perrancourt Playful came into the picture and broke the breed record by winning thirty-four CCs and thirty Best of Breeds. Playful was Top Dog All Breeds in 1979. A great showlady, she completely dominated the Airedale ring from June 1978 to Crufts 1980. She won in all ten groups, two Best in Show All Breeds and three Reserve Best in Show All Breeds and these wins gave her the title Dog of the Year 1979. American Ch. Turith Adonis was the sire of Playful

Ch. Loudwell Starlight – the top winning Airedale bitch for 1972. One of the ten champions bred and owned by Mrs Jean Campbell. Jean bred a champion from her first litter and all subsequent litters have been line bred to that dog, Ch. Loudwell Commando. This kennel has exported many dogs worldwide – to Australia in particular where there are seven Loudwells with their titles.

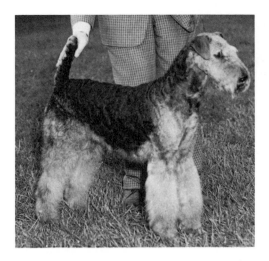

Ch. Margarite of Burdale was owned handled and prepared by George Dale all through her career. She won twelve consecutive CC's, ten with Best of Breed, three Terrier Groups, to win her Champion status in thirteen days. Bath, National Terrier and Glasgow, under Joe Braddon, Joe Green and Joe Cartledge. This photograph was taken when she was Best Bitch in Show at Windsor under Fred Cross.

Ch. Optimist of Mynair on the right and his brother 'Oscar' on the left. After winning five classes at Crufts in 1970 between them Oscar was sold to Germany that day and Optimist went on to win fourteen CC's and Best of Breeds and was the second Best Dog of All Breeds in 1970. He won his last Best of Breed at Crufts in 1972 before leaving for a very successful show career in America and Canada. Optimist and Oscar are seen here with Mavis Lodge. Mavis still has the Mynair Airedales and is a sought-after judge of great repute. She is also the President of the National Airedale Terrier Association.

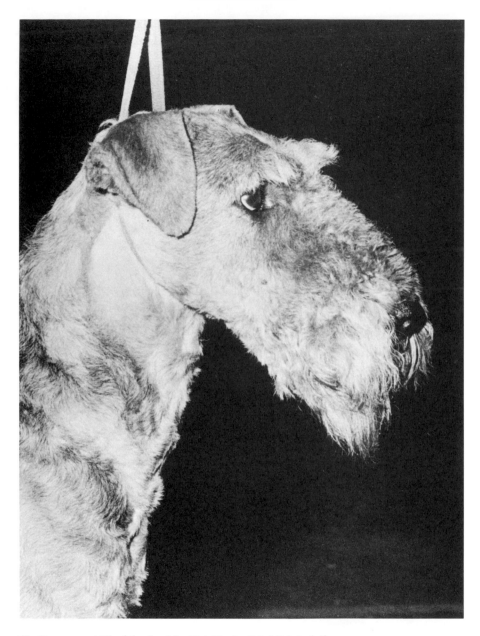

Ch. Perrancourt Playful – bred by Dot Hanks, this bitch took the show ring by storm when ace handler Ernest Sharpe campaigned her from June 1978 to end of 1979 making her Top Dog All Breeds for that year. Playful was Best of Breed at Crufts in 1979 and 1980.

and she was twice mated back to her paternal grandfather Ch. Siccawei Galliard. From these matings there were two English Champions, Perrancourt Play the Game at Jokyl, and Perrancourt Pirate who is now doing well at stud in Denmark. Ch. Siccawei Galliard emerged in the eighties as a great stud dog siring seventeen British champions.

Recent Successes

The last ten years have been very exciting for our breed in the UK with many Group and Best in Show winners including, of course, in 1986 Best in Show at Crufts, the most famous dog show in the world. In 1980 Ch. Bengal Sahib was the top Airedale Terrier in England winning four Groups, one Best in Show and two Reserve Best in Show All Breeds. Sadly this was to be Mollie Harmsworth's last champion as she died on July 29th 1981. Bengal Sahib was Best of Breed at Crufts in 1981 and went on to win eleven more CCs in that year. He was however beaten for the title of Best Airedale Terrier by Glentops Krackerjack who won two Groups and one Best in Show. This very

Ch. Glentops Krackerjack (left), Beryl McCallum's first Champion and a Best in Show winner. Unfortunately his early demise in 1983 deprived the breed of the services of this very sound and usefully bred dog. He and Ch. Bengal Sahib (right) were great rivals in 1981 changing places many times. Sahib was bred from a direct line of Bengal Champion dogs (some of these were English, some American and some champions in both countries). Sahib was Top Terrier in 1980.

143

sound dog sired three English champions one of which, Ch. Glentops Ocean Breeze, was made up in 1981. He also sired Germany's top winning dog for 1981 and 1983 before his untimely death in 1983 at the very young age of five years. His sire was Ch. Turith Brigand, full brother to Adonis, and it is sad that his early death meant that many leading breeders were not able to use him at stud. Jokyl fully intended to, but who could have guessed that his life would be so short.

Crufts in 1982 began a great run for Mynair Silver Sunbeam who won seventeen CCs, ten Best of Breeds, six Terrier Groups and one Reserve Best in Show All Breeds. Mynair Silver Sunbeam was sired by Mavis and Arthur Lodge's import, Swedish Ch. Copperstone Hannibal Hayes and she became second Top Terrier in 1982. Other bitches to be made up were Jokyl Buttons 'n' Bows and Jokyl Hot Gossip of Hillcross. The top male in 1982 was Ch. Saredon Super Trouper with

Swedish Champion Ragtime Hot Jazz. Owned and bred by Sweden's 'Father of the Breed' Stig Ahlberg, Hot Jazz is a winner of a Kennel Club Best in Show and several groups, and is just one of many home-bred Ragtime champions. Stig Ahlberg has taken many great Airedale Terriers from these shores and was the proud owner of Ch. Drakehall Dinah when she won Best in Show at the Centenary Show in 1976 at Scarborough.

fifteen CCs, eleven Best of Breeds and one Group win. Krackerjack took two more CCs and Sahib one; Turith Echelon of Saredon and Jokyl Smart Enough also gained their titles.

1983 was undoubtedly the Year of the Airedale with Ch. Jokyl Gallipants carrying all before him, winning twelve Groups, seven Best in Show All Breeds, two Reserve Best in Show and Best in Show at the National Terrier Championship Show. Gallipants was Top Dog All Breeds by a huge margin and he also won a hot Pro Dogs competition. Bitches on the other hand produced six champions; the first, Ginger Veronica was bred in Italy from English parents and brought to the UK to be shown. She was followed by Loudwell Nosegay, Jokyl Swanky Pants and Jokyl Hot Lips owned by Dodo Sandahl and later taken by her to Sweden where she became the Top Airedale for 1984. Jetstream Summer Moon became Jeanne Sarjeant's first Champion and Glentops Ocean Mist was also made up in 1983. In 1984 Gallipants was Best of Breed at Crufts and in the last four of the Terrier Group, he won the Contest of Champions (winning a colour TV for his owners) and the Pedigree Chum Champion Stakes Finals. Later in the year he took the Terrier Group at Windsor and again at Bournemouth where he went on to Reserve Best in Show. Gallipants was again Top Airedale for 1984 and won Best of Breed at Crufts in 1985 which was his last show and where he was again in the last four of the Terrier Group. Gallipants was top Airedale sire 1985, and top Terrier sire 1986.

The sire of Ch. Jokyl Gallipants was Ch. Siccawei Galliard who sired more English Airedale Terrier Champions (seventeen) than any other post-war dog, and his dam was Ch. Jokyl Smartie Pants who was dam of seven English champions, which is another record. Only one other dog achieved his title in 1983 and that was The Deerhunter of Saredon. Other winners in 1984 were Gallipants' full brother Jokyl Sunday Best, his half brother Perrancourt Pirate and Cocas Cosmos. The Deerhunter won four more CCs. In the bitches Ruth Millar's Karudon Kalypso won seven CCs and Shadli Classy Charmer won nine. Glentops Raggity Ann and Perrancourt Play the Game of Jokyl were also made up.

1985 was another terrific year for Airedales with Ch. Ginger Xmas Carol starting the year by winning the Bitch CC at Crufts, to be beaten for Best of Breed by Gallipants. The next Championship Show was at Manchester where Ginger Xmas Carol was Best in Show. She went on to win a total of fourteen Terrier Groups, four Best in Show and two Reserve Best in Show All Breeds and Reserve Best in Show at the National Terrier Show. The one other bitch to gain her title in 1985

*Ch. Karudon Kalypso. Ruth and Donald Millar's first champion.
'Libby' won her first CC at Crufts 1984. Her total number of
CCs was seven which included Best in Show at the National
Airedale Terrier Association's Championship Show.*

was Ch. Junaken Valldeb. Ten different dogs won CCs but no dog
managed to win Best of Breed. Two dogs emerged as top dogs: Ch.
Jimwin Jackpot and Ch. Saredon the Jazzsinger each with six CCs. Ch.
Elbana Prairie and Ch. Shadli Fantom also gained their titles. The
breed received a great boost at the beginning of 1986 when Ch. Ginger
Xmas Carol won Best in Show at Crufts exactly twenty-five years after
Tweedsbairn's great win. This was to be her last show and what a
way to retire! For dogs the rest of the season was divided between Ch.
Saredon the Jazzsinger with fourteen CCs and Ch. Stargus Sea King
with seven. In the bitches classes Ch. Jokyl Vivacious and Ch.
Something Special for Jokyl each won six CCs with Something Special
taking the Terrier Group at Southern Counties. Other bitch Champions
made up were Junaken Vanity, Beacytan Gay Paree and Beacytan
Koh-i-Nor. Jazzsinger and Sea King won more CCs in 1987 and
the interesting import American Ch. Blackjacks Nostradamus was
awarded five CCs. The biggest winner of the year however, was

Ch. Stargus Sea King. Mrs Lesley Lee's first champion. Bred, prepared and handled by her throughout his career Sea King won his qualifying CC at Crufts in 1986. The ladies have certainly come into their own in the show ring now.

Saredon Handyman with eleven Challenge Certificates and a Terrier Group win. Something Special took two more CCs and the Junaken bitches, Valetta, Vee Jay and Vallotta of Beacytan achieved champion status as did Dendaric Figurehead in 1987.

1988 failed to produce a single Group winner although Handyman won a further fourteen CCs. Ch. Glentops Trick or Treat had six Certificates and Ch. Shadli Magnum of Robroyd was also made up. In this year eleven different bitches shared the twenty-eight Challenge Certificates which were offered with Ch. Junaken Veni Vedi Vici and Ch. Saredon September Morn being the second and third Jazzsinger offspring to be made up. Ch. Jokyl American Dream and Ch. Beacytan Serendipity were the first of Nostradamus progeny to gain their titles and Bob Gould made up his first Champion, the home-bred Broen Eyebury Princess. American Dream was the top winning bitch in 1988. Handyman took six more certificates in 1989 and seemed set fair to eclipse Playful's record of thirty-four CCs but left for Japan before achieving the record. Handyman's chief opponent Ch. Jokyl Hillcross Hotshot, the eleventh English champion sired by Gallipants won ten CCs, one Terrier Group and two Group seconds. That year saw Florac King of Scots at Stargus (now in the United States), Ballintober Gold of Saredon and Beacytan Troubadour also take their titles. A record

Ch. Saredon Handyman – bred by Judy Averis who specializes in producing big winning males. Handyman holds the record for the number of CCs won by a male (32). (Previously held by Ch. Tanworth Merriment.) He was Top Airedale Terrier in 1987 and 1988.

number of seven bitches became champions in 1989, four of them sired by Nostradamus. These were Jokyl Liberty Lady, Jokyl What a Gem (ex Jokyl Buttons 'n' Bows, dam of American Dream), Beacytan Vanilla, McKerros Caledonian Girl George Dale's Codale Margarite, Broen Apple of my Eye and the last Champion of the year Jokyl Something Else made up the seven. Nostradamus was top Airedale Terrier sire of 1988 and again in 1989 when he shared the honours with Gallipants. We look forward to the future with the possibility of more imports.

Influence from Overseas

Overseas there have been many Airedale Terriers famous in their own countries. American breeders have produced some wonderful home-breds. American Ch. Finlair Tiger of Stoneridge, Finlair Isis and the latest star Tartans Oil Patch Star are just a few. Argentina have some really top quality stock, and they are able to take a combination of

A famous dog in the 'Blue Peter' television studio.

English and American lines which is really putting them on the map. Australia has some very active Airedale Terrier Clubs and despite the long distance and awesome cost of air fares, some stalwarts have imported top class dogs. Most of them were from Burdale, Siccawei, Bengal, Loudwell and Jokyl. One very interesting import in the seventies was Drakehall Dragoon – brother of the centenary winning 'Dinah'. The Australian breeders are so enthusiastic, travel long distances to exhibit their dogs, and invite judges from all over the world to officiate at their shows. For many years Sweden has had top class Airedale Terriers, with many of the best of British going there. Stig Ahlberg's Ragtime Kennel has imported many dogs over the years, mainly from Krescent and Bengal, and has been a great promoter of Airedale Terriers in Sweden, encouraging many young people in their interest with the breed. Finnish interest is keen owing much to Pirjo Hjelm of Big Lady's fame.

There are inevitably many wonderful dogs and breeders who have been left out of this chapter due to lack of space, and it is a subject worthy of a book of its own.

149

Appendix 1

Champions from 1946 to the Present Day

Name	D.O.B.	Sex	Sire	Dam	Breeder	Owner
1946						
Ch. Foxdenton Topscore	14.6.44	B	Talena Majestic	Moelwyn Princess	E. Roberts	Miss G.M. Hilton
1947						
Ch. Aislaby Elzevia	1.9.45	B	Mottos Walstow President	Aislaby Eldgyth	Mrs G. Hayes	Mrs N. Hayes
Ch. Brineland Barrier	10.5.45	D	Orfordane War Venture	Coppertops Girl	H. Pace	J.E. Watson
Ch. Holmbury Bandit	1.8.43	D	Berrycroft Atoppa	Berrycroft Aruta	Mrs A.J. Hopwood	Major J.H. Wright
Ch. Murraysgate Minstrel	27.7.45	D	Chathall Newsboy	Murraysgate Winniedale	J. Kerr	Breeder
Ch. Raimon Rhapsody	8.12.42	B	Waycon Designer	Miss Cherchyl	Mrs R.E. Haslam	Breeder
Ch. Rural Wyrewood Apollo	16.6.45	D	Solo Aristocrat	Wyrewood Siccawei Pictorial	Miss E. Woods	Mrs H. Care
Ch. Talena Brittania	14.6.44	B	Talena Majestic	Moelwyn Princess	E. Roberts	Mrs A.L. Holloway
1948						
Ch. Atanta of Aes	16.3.44	B	Murraysgate Man O'War	Wynadale Whatagift	J. Gray	Mrs F. Whyte
Ch. Berrycroft Bedlam Bruce	28.3.45	D	Eastthorpe Nicholas	Howcliffe Jacqueline	Mrs E.F. Dawson	Mrs A.J. Hopwood
Ch. Chip of Lancooross	11.5.46	D	Ch. Holmbury Bandit	Lady of Lancooross	W.H. Cooper	Breeder
Ch. Foxdenton Wightwick Major	18.3.46	D	Chathall Newsboy	Pride of Wistaria	W.E. Hindley	E. Holme

Name	Date	Sex	Sire	Dam	Owner	Breeder
Ch. Garthwood Courtfield Cadess	12.12.44	B	Talena Majestic	Courtfield Orchid	B.Y. Wilson	T.S. Wood & J. Atkinson
Ch. Glenmavis Geisha	12.7.46	B	His Lordship of Tullochard	Glenmavis Gracie	J. Williamson	Mrs J. Williamson
Ch. Holmbury Brenda	7.8.46	B	Ch. Holmbury Bandit	Aireton Honey Child	C.E.D. Batt	Mrs M.E. Ohm
Ch. Murraysgate Mustang	26.12.44	D	Chathall Newsboy	Murraysgate Merriment	J. Kerr	W. Fielden
Ch. Patricia of Handforth	17.2.46	B	Watlyn Aristocrat	Bridgemill Duno	Mrs I. Millett	Mrs G. Nowell
Ch. Penelope of Joreen	16.5.47	B	Ch. Rural Wyrewood Apollo	Onyx of Joreen	Mrs J.C. Coghlan	Breeder
Ch. Siccawei Wizard	27.1.46	D	Talena Majestic	Siccawei Preses	Mrs C. Halford	Breeder

1949

Name	Date	Sex	Sire	Dam	Owner	Breeder
Ch. Chathall Caliban	12.5.44	D	Bankhouse Spitfire	Chathall Miranda	F.E.P. Chatterton	J.B. Plant
Ch. Foxdenton Topliner	3.3.47	D	Solo Aristocrat	Foxdenton Topscore	Miss G.M. Hilton	Breeder
Ch. Murose Replica	15.4.46	D	Ch. Holmbury Bandit	Mulrose Lassie	W.H. Brampton	Major J. Wright
Ch. Murraysgate Merrijoe	23.9.47	D	Bring Luck	Murraysgate Winniedale	J. Kerr	Breeder
Ch. Airebank Queen	12.1.47	B	Chathall Newsboy	Airebank Girl	F. Bentham	Breeder
Ch. Holmbury Terrapin Trix	20.6.46	B	Ch. Holmbury Bandit	Fritchley Brunette	B.H. Tipping	V. Hardie
Ch. Lass O'the Main	10.10.47	B	Ch. Murraysgate Minstrel	Murraysgate Maydonna	W. Reville	J.S. Buchan
Ch. Phoebe of Joreen	16.5.47	B	Ch. Rural Wyrewood Apollo	Onyx of Joreen	Mrs J.E. Coghlan	Breeder
Ch. Siccawei Zarina	2.7.47	B	Ch. Rural Wyrewood Apollo	Siccawei Preses	Mrs C.M. Halford	Breeder

1950

Name	Date	Sex	Sire	Dam	Owner	Breeder
Ch. Bamfylde Knight	4.5.49	D	Stalena Statesman	Springtime Enchantress	Mrs E.A. Halliday	Breeder
Ch. Barton of Burdale	26.7.48	D	Lineside Marquis of Burdale	Beamland Pamela of Burdale	Miss E.M. Jones	Breeder
Ch. Riverina Reunion	20.3.47	D	Westhay Alliance	Riverina Riot	Misses P. & S. McCaughey	Breeder
Ch. Son of Merrijack	9.3.48	D	Holmbury Murraysgate Merrijak	Nelson Inn Lassie	G.H. Breakwell	Breeder
Ch. Weycroft Wyldboy	8.4.49	D	Ch. Holmbury Bandit	Judy of Peolshall	S.T. Croome	T. Brampton
Ch. Alexia of Yellowhills	24.11.48	B	Ch. Siccawei Wizard	Josephine of Milnerwhit	Capt & Mrs F.P. Shannon	Mrs F.P. Shannon
Ch. Dunelm Wondrous	7.7.48	B	Stantham Mascot	Dunelm Princess	T. McHugh	Breeder

Name	D.O.B.	Sex	Sire	Dam	Breeder	Owner
Ch. Handforth Princess	21.12.48	B	Ch. Rural Wyrewood Apollo	Patricia of Handforth	Mrs G. Nowell	Mrs D. Morrison
Ch. Mellish Melanie	7.6.48	B	Ch. Murraysgate Minstrel	Mellish Melisa	Miss G. Rogers	Breeder
Ch. Mellish Melody	7.6.48	B	Ch. Murraysgate Minstrel	Mellish Melisa	Miss G. Rogers	H. Nock
Ch. Weycroft Wondrous	8.4.49	B	Ch. Holmbury Bandit	Judy of Peolshall	S.J. Croome	T. Brampton

1951

Name	D.O.B.	Sex	Sire	Dam	Breeder	Owner
Ch. Bertram of Burdale	26.7.48	D	Lineside Marquis of Burdale	Beamland Pamela of Burdale	Miss E.M. Jones	C. Poole
Ch. Crossdale Aristocrat	29.8.50	D	Ch. Weycroft Wyldboy	Crossbye Kimby	Mrs O. Wales	Breeder
Ch. Dunelm Mascot	13.1.47	D	Stanham Mascot	Dunelm Princess	T. McHugh	Breeder
Ch. Hamish of Joreen	15.1.50	D	Ch. Murraysgate Minstrel	Ch. Phoebe of Joreen	Mrs J.C. Coghlan	Breeder
Ch. Murraysgate Maestro	18.5.49	D	Ch. Murraysgate Minstrel	Murraysgate Millings	J. Kerr	Breeder
Ch. Watforth Aristocrat	22.5.48	D	Handforth Pedr	Ideal	Mr & Mrs W. Key	Mr & Mrs J. Wild
Ch. Bengal Ballydam	29.3.49	D	Aislaby Hawk	Bengal Brilliant	M.E. Harmsworth	A. Toye
Ch. Britannia of Burdale	26.7.48	B	Linesman Marquis of Burdale	Beamland Pamela of Burdale	Miss E.M. Jones	Breeder
Ch. Mottos Gipsey Princess	9.4.48	B	Talena Majestic	Mottos Lady Selwyn	B. Kronfield	J.E. Mottrom
Ch. St Malo Merry Maid	26.2.48	B	Ch. Chip of Lancooross	Siccawei Xample	A. Kendall	G.F. Holden
Ch. Warstock Princess	30.5.49	B	Ch. Chip of Lancooross	Siccawei Xample	A. Kendall	G. Fantom

1952

Name	D.O.B.	Sex	Sire	Dam	Breeder	Owner
Ch. Bengal Bengali	14.4.50	D	Ch. Son of Merrijak	Ch. Benal Ballydam	M.E. Harmsworth	Breeder
Ch. Cardinal of Joreen	21.7.50	D	Ch. Murraysgate Minstrel	Wonder of Joreen	J.C. Coghcan	Breeder
Ch. Kenelm Makeway	30.5.49	D	Ch. Chip of Lancooross	Siccawei Xample	A. Kendall	J.W. Bywater
Ch. Kresent Samuel	7.3.51	D	Ch. Barton of Burdale	Kresent Tzygone	Mrs D. Hodgkinson	Mr T. Hodgkinson & Mrs E. Bridge
Ch. Robroy of Joreen	15.1.50	D	Ch. Murraysgate Minstrel	Ch. Phoebe of Joreen	J.C. Coghlan	P. Coxwell & Mrs N. Mote
Ch. Solo Tiger Rag	14.4.50	D	Solo Aristocrat	Boniface of Smethmont	Miss D.M. Perry	J.E. Turner
Ch. Southkirk Monarch	9.2.50	D	Ch. Murraysgate Minstrel	Ch. Lass O'The Main	J.S. Buchan	Breeder
Ch. Deridonian Replica	29.12.49	B	Ch. Murose Replica	Lady Craig	H. Owen	M.J. Davies
Ch. Gosmore Dalehall Dainty Miss	21.5.50	B	Ch. Son of Merrijak	Haldys Avoca	Mrs G. Heath	Mr & Mrs S.W. Dallison

Name	Date	Sex	Sire	Dam	Owner	Breeder
Ch. Riverina Bewitched	10.3.50	B	Ch. Riverina Reunion	Tridwr Milady	P. & S. McCaughey	Breeders
Ch. Rosalind of Tullochard	23.3.49	B	Ch. Murraysgate Mustang	Diana of Lijaneth	Mrs H.S. Gates	J. Hardie jnr
Ch. Searchlight Pride of Gwen	30.5.49	B	Ch. Chip of Lancooross	Siccawei Xample	Mrs A. Kendall	Mrs M. Kington
Ch. Siccawei Ideal	13.9.50	B	Ch. Riverina Reunion	Siccawei Preses	C.M. Halford	Breeder
Ch. Tycroit Caprice of Joreen	21.7.50	B	Ch. Murraysgate Minstrel	Wonder of Joreen	J.C. Coghlan	A.M. Jenkinson
Ch. Weycroft Wishful	5.4.49	B	Ch. Holmbury Bandit	Judy of Peolshall	S.T. Croome	T. Brampton

1953

Name	Date	Sex	Sire	Dam	Owner	Breeder
Ch. Collipriest Stormer	26.4.52	D	Ch. Rural Wyrewood Apollo	Collipriest Brownleaf	Mrs W. Pincott	Breeder
Ch. Dovedale Crusader	23.5.51	D	Dovedale Bluebird Aeriel	Dovedale Revival	H.E. Thomas	Breeder
Ch. Haldys Field Marshall	25.12.50	D	Lineside Marquis of Burdale	Haldys Avoca	Mrs G. Heath	Breeder
Ch. Hamish of Glenbeth	17.11.51	D	Ch. Barton of Burdale	Carol of Joreen	J. Speed	Breeder
Ch. Cactus Blossom	8.10.48	B	Ch. Cactus	Cactus Candy Baloups	C.F. Ephraim	Maj W.D. Cargill
Ch. Kresent Sincerity	7.3.51	B	Ch. Barton of Burdale	Kresent Tzygone	D. Hodgkinson	Breeder
Ch. Quayton Adorable	16.9.51	B	Ch. Bamfylde Knight	Wistful of Joreen	W.F. Quick	Breeder

1954

Name	Date	Sex	Sire	Dam	Owner	Breeder
Ch. Dorrihill Gay Batchelor	4.7.52	D	Bostock of Burdale	Handforth Princess	D.A. Morrison	Breeder
Ch. Searchlight Defiance	31.8.52	D	Ch. Rural Wyrewood Apollo	Ch. Searchlight Pride of Gwen	Mrs M. Kington	Mr & Mrs S. Hughes
Ch. Senator of Joreen	8.9.51	D	Ch. Hamish of Joreen	Wonder of Joreen	J.C. Coghlan	J.C. Coghlan & M. Murray
Ch. Acter of Mynair	2.6.53	B	Ch. Krescent Samuel	Dinah of Yellowhills	A. Lodge	Breeder
Ch. Riverina Encore	17.1.52	B	Ch. Riverina Reunion	Riverina Vogue	P. McCaughey & Mrs D. Schuth	Miss D. Sedorski
Ch. Siccawei Mannequin	30.5.52	B	Siccawei Jester	Siccawei Iolanthe	Mrs C.M. Halford	I. Galliers
Ch. Tycroit Tinkerbell	11.8.52	B	Ch. Murraysgate Maestro	Tycroit Caprice of Joreen	A.M. Jenkinson	Breeder

1955

Name	Date	Sex	Sire	Dam	Owner	Breeder
Ch. Bengal Newydd Sonnyboy	20.1.53	D	Rural Paladin of Joreen	Lady Bengough	Mrs B. Page	M.E. Harmsworth
Ch. Gosmore Talked About	22.8.53	D	Ch. Gosmore Attack	Ch. Gosmore Dalehall Dainty Miss	G.W. Dallison	Breeder

Name	D.O.B.	Sex	Sire	Dam	Breeder	Owner
Ch. Tycroit Tosca	19.2.54	D	Tycroit Hilsam Highnote	Coronation Princess	A.M. Jenkinson	Breeder
Ch. Tycroit Tulyar	24.3.53	D	Tycroit Hilsam Highnote	Tycroit Caprice of Joreen	A.M. Jenkinson	A. Scott
Ch. Westhay Jamus	8.2.53	D	Raimon Nobbler of Normarsh	Westhay Souvenir	Mrs I.E. Hayes	S.J. Hayes
Ch. Collipriest Enchantress	22.3.53	B	Rural Paladins Son	Collipriest Brown Leaf	Mrs E. Pincott	Breeder
Ch. Riverina Diana of Siccawei	20.5.54	B	Riverina Siccawei Phoebus	Ch. Riverina Bewitched	Miss P. McCaughy & Mrs D. Schuth	C.M. Halford
Ch. Siccawei Olympic	24.10.52	B	Westhay Alliance	Siccawei Zarina	C.M. Halford	Breeder
Ch. Tycroit Glenbina	15.7.53	B	Lineside Marquis of Burdale	Carol of Joreen	B. & J. Speed	Miss A. Scott
1956						
Ch. Radcliffe Celebrity	14.3.53	D	Boris of Burdale	Dinkie of Yellowhills	T. Probert	Breeder
Ch. Riverina Siccawei Phoebus	28.2.53	D	Ch. Rural Wyrewood Apollo	Ch. Siccawei Ideal	Mrs C.M. Halford	Miss P. McCaughey & Mrs D. Schuth
Ch. Tycroit Tempo	25.3.55	D	Tycroit Tomkins	Tycroit Treble	A.M. Jenkinson	Breeder
Ch. Quayton Cherie	29.5.54	B	Ch. Collipriest Stormer	Ch. Quayton Adorable	W.F. Quick	W.N. Robinson
Ch. Riverina Dryad	29.5.52	B	Ch. Riverina Siccawei Phoebus	Riverina Bewitched	Miss P. McCaughey & Mrs D. Schuth	Breeders
Ch. Riverina Westhay Flayre	6.2.53	B	Ch. Rural Wyrewood Apollo	Riverina Bewitched	Mrs I.E. Hayes	Miss P. McCaughey & Mrs D. Schuth
Ch. Westhay Fiona	21.9.54	B	Ch. Westhay Jamus	Ch. Riverina Westhay Flayre	Mrs I.E. Hayes	Mrs I.E. Hayes & Miss N. Haslam
1957						
Ch. Bengal Collipriest Diplomat	1.1.56	D	Ch. Collipriest Stormer	Rural Reverie	Mrs H. Care	Mrs M. Harmsworth
Ch. Riverina Tweed	1.3.54	D	Ch. Riverina Reunion	Riverina Vogue	Miss P. McCaughey & Mrs D. Schuth	Breeders
Ch. Sanbrook Sandpiper	22.5.55	D	Highfield Briar	Sue of Guildford	Mrs L.E. Marshall	Breeder
Ch. Braknight Riverina Garnet	4.7.55	B	Riverina Yorick	Riverina Bewitched	Miss P. McCaughey & Mrs D. Schuth	A. Bradshaw
Ch. Riverina Galena	4.7.55	B	Riverina Yorick	Riverina Bewitched	Miss P. McCaughey & Mrs D. Schuth	Breeders

Name	Date	Sex	Sire	Dam	Owner	Breeder
Ch. Searchlight Pandora	14.11.53	B	Rural Paladins Son	Ch. Searchlight Pride of Gwen	Mrs M. Kington	Breeder
Ch. Shaftmoor Sapphire	6.10.55	B	Searchlight Sovereign	Ch. Warstock Princess	G. Fantom	Mrs M. Lloyd

1958

Name	Date	Sex	Sire	Dam	Owner	Breeder
Ch. Burgmer of Burdale	7.2.57	D	Judicious Juggler	Mischief of Burdale	Miss E.M. Jones	Breeder
Ch. Haldys Re-Echo	27.12.56	D	Tithebarn Tycroit Tandit	Tycroit Titania	W. Bentley	Mrs G. Heath
Ch. Mayjack Briar	24.9.55	D	Ch. Riverina Siccawei Phoebus	Cummock Jacqueline	Mr G. Jackson	Breeder
Ch. Bengal Kresent Duchess	7.4.57	B	Ch. Bengal Collipriest Diplomat	Kresent Model Maid	Mrs D. Hodgkinson	Mrs M. Harmsworth
Ch. Springtime of Rangefield	26.6.56	B	Ch. Gosmore Talked About	Lady Luck of Rangefield	Mrs C.M. Hook	Breeder
Ch. Taywen Revelations	20.5.55	B	Highfield Briar	Lineside Melody	J. Shufflebotham	Miss W. Taylor

1959

Name	Date	Sex	Sire	Dam	Owner	Breeder
Ch. Hartington Havoc of Tycroit	25.10.57	D	Ch. Tycroit Tempo	Soxers Final Result	P.R. Devlin	Miss A.M. Jenkinson
Ch. Jokyl Berrieslea Monarch	4.12.55	D	Edstone Monarch	Newsboy's Lassie	J.L. Stanley	G. Jackson
Ch. Lanewood Lysander	15.8.57	D	Ch. Riverina Siccawei Phoebus	Ch. Quayton Cherie	W.N. Robinson	Breeder
Ch. Riverina Maraschino	24.10.56	D	Riverina Esquire	Riverina Driad	Miss P. McCaughey & Mrs D. Schuth	Miss J. Bancroft Livingstone
Ch. Gosmore Bengal Sari	22.12.57	B	Ch. Bengal Collipriest Diplomat	Mendip Melody	Mrs M. Harmsworth	Breeder
Ch. Jokyl Firefly	1.1.58	B	Ch. Mayjack Briar	Ch. Riverina Galena	G. Jackson	Breeder
Ch. Moorlyn Kresent Delight	7.4.57	B	Ch. Bengal Collipriest Diplomat	Kresent Model Maid	Mrs D. Hodgkinson	Mrs R.A. Lloyd

1960

Name	Date	Sex	Sire	Dam	Owner	Breeder
Ch. Riverina Tweedsbairn	29.1.58	D	Ch. Riverina Tweed	Ch. Riverina Diana of Siccawei	Mrs C.M. Halford	Miss P. McCaughey & Mrs D. Schuth
Ch. Searchlight Trubadore	2.7.58	D	Searchlight Defiance	Wrayside Gilly	Mrs A. Coutts	Mrs M. Kington
Ch. Cortina of Mynair	14.7.57	B	Westfen Cavalier	Ace of Mynair	A. Lodge	Breeder
Ch. Jokyl Ballysauce	1.1.58	B	Ch. Mayjack Briar	Ch. Riverina Galena	G. Jackson	Breeder
Ch. Moorlyn Kresent Fiona	26.2.59	B	Bengal Sabu	Kresent Model Maid	Mrs D. Hodgkinson	Mrs R. Lloyd

Name	D.O.B.	Sex	Sire	Dam	Breeder	Owner
Ch. Riverina Amanda	1.10.56	B	Ch. Riverina Siccawei Phoebus	Ch. Riverina Bewitched	Miss P. McCaughey & Mrs D. Schuth	Breeders
Ch. Riverina Quadrille	19.4.57	B	Ch. Riverina Siccawei Phoebus	Ch. Riverina Encore	Miss P. McCaughey & Mrs D. Schuth	Breeders
Ch. Siccawei Artemis	18.5.57	B	Siccawei Marquis	Riverina Diana of Siccawei	Mrs C.M. Halford	Breeder
1961						
Ch. Bengal Kresent Brave	23.4.60	D	Bengal Bladud	Kresent Model Maid	Mrs D. Hodgkinson	Mrs M.E. Harmsworth
Ch. Kresent Bonny Boy	23.4.60	D	Bengal Bladud	Kresent Model Maid	Mrs D. Hodgkinson	Breeder
Ch. Raimon Robert the Bruce	21.10.58	D	Ch. Riverina Tweed	Raimon Regal	Miss N. Haslam	Breeder
Ch. Gosmore Kresent Karneval	20.9.59	B	Kresent Leonertes	Kresent Model Maid	Mrs D. Hodgkinson	Mrs A.B. Dallison
Ch. Jokyl Top of the Form	7.5.59	B	Turkish Rural Cavalier	Chippinghey Deep Loam	G. Jackson	Breeder
Ch. Riverina Siccawei Diadem	29.1.58	B	Ch. Riverina Tweed	Ch. Riverina Diadem of Siccawei	Mrs C.M. Halford	Mrs A.B. Watson
1962						
Ch. Jokyl Bengal Figaro	9.5.61	D	Ch. Bengal Kresent Brave	Bengal Chippinghey Fircone	Mrs M.E. Harmsworth	G. Jackson
Ch. Riverina Balquhidder Bairn	29.4.60	D	Ch. Riverina Tweedsbairn	Ch. Taywen Revelation	Miss W. Taylor	Miss P. McCaughey & Mrs D. Schuth
Ch. Bengal Kresent Ballerina	23.4.60	B	Bengal Bladud	Kresent Model Maid	Mrs D. Hodgkinson	Mrs M.E. Harmsworth
Ch. Fortina of Mynair	16.12.60	B	Kresent Diplomat	Cortina of Mynair	A. Lodge	Breeder
Ch. Jokyl Chippinghey Greensleeves	1.7.58	B	Turkish Rural Cavalier	Chippinghey Briar Rose	Miss M. Ing	G. Jackson
Ch. Kresent Beloved	23.4.60	B	Bengal Bladud	Kresent Model Maid	Mrs D. Hodgkinson	Breeder
Ch. Riverina Berwick Maid	29.1.60	B	Ch. Riverina Tweedsbairn	Ch. Taywen Revelation	W. Taylor	Miss P. McCaughey & Mrs D. Schuth
Ch. Siccawei Humdinger	27.7.59	B	Ch. Riverina Tweedsbairn	Joyeuse of Siccawei	Mrs C.M. Halford	Breeder
1963						
Ch. Jokyl Bengal Lionheart	12.2.62	D	Bengal Skipper of Limebell	Bengal Chippinghey Fircone	Mrs M.E. Harmsworth	G. Jackson

Name	Date	Sex	Sire	Dam	Owner	Breeder
Ch. Kresent Gay Gordon	4.1.62	D	Bengal Skipper of Limebell	Kresent Model Maid	Mrs D. Hodgkinson	Breeder
Ch. Wynadale Ensign of Mynair	12.5.60	D	Brunel of Mynair	Cortina of Mynair	A. Lodge	Mrs A.B. Dallison
Ch. Margarite of Burdale	27.7.61	B	Marcus of Burdale	Astoria of Ravensmoel	W. Dodd	G. Dale
Ch. Siccawei Princess Pam	8.9.61	B	Ch. Riverina Tweedsbairn	Ch. Siccawei Artemis	Mrs C.M. Halford	Breeder

1964

Name	Date	Sex	Sire	Dam	Owner	Breeder
Ch. Grenadier of Mynair	27.4.63	D	Brunel of Mynair	Ch. Cortina of Mynair	A. Lodge	Breeder
Ch. Jokyl Lane	16.11.62	D	Ch. Mayjack Briar	Jokyl Tonic	Mr & Mrs G. Jackson	Breeders
Ch. Jokyl Othello von Kirm	12.1.62	D	Etzel von Kirm	Hera von Kirm	M.R. Tegelar	Mr & Mrs G. Jackson
Ch. Riverina Benedictine	23.1.61	D	Ch. Riverina Tweedsbairn	Riverina Wayward Witch	Miss P. McCaughey & Mrs D. Schuth	Miss P. McCaughey & Mrs D. Schuth & Mrs M. Cartledge
Ch. Bengal Begum	10.6.63	B	Bengal Leander	Bengal Kresent Ballerina	Mrs M.E. Harmsworth	Breeder
Ch. Brulyn Breeze	16.4.62	B	Bengal Kresent Brave	Brulyn Brimful	Mrs M.D. Bishop	Mrs A.K. Hunt
Ch. Jokyl Queen of Space	23.7.62	B	Ch. Jokyl Bengal Figaro	Ch. Jokyl Top of the Form	G. Jackson	Breeder
Ch. Jokyl Solitaire	21.8.61	B	Turkish Rural Cavalier	Ch. Jokyl Ballysauce	G. Jackson	B. Morris
Ch. Kresent Glorious	4.1.62	B	Bengal Skipper of Limebell	Kresent Model Maid	Mrs D. Hodgkinson	Breeder
Ch. Tanworth Beryl of Burdale	31.3.61	B	Tornado of Tanworth	Mischief of Burdale	E.M. Jones	Mr & Mrs J. Holland

1965

Name	Date	Sex	Sire	Dam	Owner	Breeder
Ch. Bengal Fastnet	9.5.61	D	Ch. Bengal Kresent Brave	Bengal Chippinghey Fircone	M.E. Harmsworth	D. Rees & W.T. Berry
Ch. Bengal Gunga Din	30.9.62	D	Ch. Bengal Kresent Brave	Bengal Chippinghey Fircone	Mrs M.E. Harmsworth	Breeder
Ch. Jokyl Space Leader	23.7.62	D	Ch. Jokyl Bengal Figaro	Ch. Jokyl Top of the Form	Mr & Mrs G. Jackson	Breeders
Ch. Loudwell Kommando	17.11.61	D	Ch. Loudwell Lysander	Loudwell Kresent Karusell	Mrs J. Campbell	Mrs J. Campbell & T. Adair
Ch. Marquis of Burdale	3.6.63	D	Sanbrook Sandpippin	Denise of Burdale	Miss E.M. Jones	Breeder
Ch. Jokyl Lodgewater Blossom	5.1.64	B	Ch. Jokyl Space Leader	Jokyl Pretty Polly	G. Blowfield	Mr & Mrs G. Jackson
Ch. Loudwell Folly	23.6.63	B	Ch. Lanewood Lysander	Bengal Fantasia	Mrs J. Campbell	Breeder
Ch. Wynadale Withit	7.11.63	B	Ch. Jokyl Space Leader	Warcry Toreign	J. Gray	Mr & Mrs Millings

Name	D.O.B.	Sex	Sire	Dam	Breeder	Owner
1966						
Ch. Bengal Brulyn Sahib	24.8.65	D	Ch. Bengal Gunga Din	Ch. Brulyn Brimful	Mrs D.M. Bishop	Mrs M.E. Harmsworth
Ch. Jokyl Eagle	8.6.65	D	Jokyl Chippinghey Kestrel	Bengal Ingrid	Miss A. Toms	Mr & Mrs G. Jackson
Ch. Mynair Eyecatcher of Wellingdale	18.10.63	D	Brunel of Mynair	Finola of Mynair	S. Lammin	A. Lodge
Ch. Ariel of Siccawei	31.3.64	B	Bengal Fastnet	Lansdown Coquette	C. Arberry	Mrs C.M. Halford
Ch. Iona of Mynair	10.11.64	B	Ch. Bengal Gunga Din	Ch. Fortina of Mynair	A. Lodge	Breeder
1967						
Ch. Bengal Mowgli	12.4.66	D	Ch. Bengal Gunga Din	Bengal Thunderbird	Mrs M.E. Harmsworth	Breeder
Ch. Searchlight Tycoon	3.11.65	D	Ch. Bengal Gunga Din	Suliston Psyche	J. Derrick	Mr & Mrs W.E. Kington
Ch. Jokyl Moon Princess	17.6.65	B	Jokyl Chippinghey Kestrel	Ch. Jokyl Queen of Space	Mr & Mrs G. Jackson	Breeders
Ch. Kresent Vanity Fair	24.8.63	B	Ch. Searchlight Troubadour	Ch. Kresent Beloved	Mrs D. Hodgkinson & S. Ahlberg	Mrs D. Hodgkinson
Ch. Tintara Classical	4.3.64	B	Ch. Bengal Fastnet	Riverina Rosemary of Tintara	Mrs P. Crome	Breeder
1968						
Ch. Jokyl Chippinghey Mallow	6.3.67	D	Jokyl Goal Keeper	Chippinghey Leafshadow	Miss M. Ing	G. Jackson
Ch. Jokyl Superman	10.10.67	D	Ch. Jokyl Space Leader	Suliston Psyche	J. Derrick	Mr & Mrs G. Jackson
Ch. Riverina Domecq	3.5.64	D	Riverina Cognac	Riverina Siccawei Diadem	Miss P. McCaughey & Mrs D. Schuth	Breeders
Ch. Bengal Springtime	25.1.65	B	Ch. Bengal Brulyn Sahib	Bengal Begum	Mrs M.E. Harmsworth	Breeder
Ch. Bernice of Burdale	1.7.65	B	Ch. Marquis of Burdale	Mabelle of Burdale	Miss E.M. Jones	D.R. Keith
Ch. Merrycroft My Fair Lady	7.11.65	B	Ch. Marquis of Burdale	Merrycroft Matilda	E.V. Baldwin & A.E. Lowther	Breeders

1969

Name	Date	Sex	Sire	Dam	Owner	Breeder
Ch. Lanewood Lombard	3.4.66	D	Ch. Bengal Gunga Din	Lanewood Kewi Oriole	Mr & Mrs Robinson	W.N. Robinson Breeder
Ch. Siccawei Kings Ransom	14.7.67	D	Ch. Bengal Fastnet	Ch. Siccawei Humdinger	Mrs C.M. Halford	Breeder
Ch. Allerdene Foinavon of Wellingdale	28.3.67	B	Ch. Indomitable of Mynair	Ch. Fortina of Mynair	S.E. Lammin	A. Lodge & Mrs A.E. Grieves
Ch. Coppercrest Wait & See	24.8.67	B	Ch. Searchlight Tycoon	Ch. Partypiece of Tanworth	Mrs P. Hollingsworth	Breeder
Ch. Edismac Day Dream	4.8.67	B	Ch. Searchlight Newstime	Ch. Brulyn Breeze	Mrs A.K. Hunt	Mrs D.M. Bishop
Ch. Siccawei Impudent Miss	20.8.66	B	Ch. Bengal Fastnet	Ch. Siccawei Princess Pam	Mrs C.M. Halford	Breeder

1970

Name	Date	Sex	Sire	Dam	Owner	Breeder
Ch. Jokyl Rudolph	18.4.64	D	Ch. Jokyl Othello von Kirm	Jokyl Top of the Form	Mr & Mrs G. Jackson	Mr & Mrs B. Morris
Ch. Optimist of Mynair	13.2.69	D	Brulyn Baha Dur	Katinka of Mynair	A. Lodge	Breeder
Ch. Bengal Suliston Merry Maid	3.11.65	B	Ch. Bengal Gunga Din	Suliston Psyche	J. Derrick	Mrs M.E. Harmsworth
Ch. Fancy Free of Tanworth	2.6.68	B	Ger Ch. Bengal Figaro	Ch. Tanworth Beryl of Burdale	Mr & Mrs J. Holland	Breeders
Ch. Jokyl Elegance	12.7.68	B	Ger Ch. Bengal Figaro	Jokyl Hera	Mrs A.L. Jones	Mr & Mrs G. Jackson
Ch. Mollygray Model of Mynair	28.4.67	B	Ch. Mynair Eyecatcher of Wellingdale	Ch. Iona of Mynair	A. Lodge	Mr & Mrs G.A. Ward
Ch. Siccawei Ruby	5.2.69	B	Siccawei Flaming Torch	Ch. Siccawei Impudent Miss	Mrs C.M. Halford	Breeder

1971

Name	Date	Sex	Sire	Dam	Owner	Breeder
Ch. Jokyl Superior	15.8.68	D	Int. Ch. Jokyl Bengal Figaro	Kenlucky Latora	Mrs A.L. Jones	Mr & Mrs G. Jackson
Ch. Siccawei Windrose	21.1.69	B	Ch. Siccawei Kings Ransome	Siccawei Jess's Postscript	Mrs C.M. Halford	Breeder
Ch. Bengal Flamboyant	20.6.63	D	Bengal Buldeo	Ch. Bengal Springtime	Mrs M. Harmsworth	Breeder
Ch. Loudwell Regal	28.5.66	B	Ch. Mynair Eyecatcher of Wellingdale	Ch. Loudwell Folly	Mrs J. Campbell	Breeder
Ch. Krescent Unique	7.9.68	D	Krescent Quando	Ch. Krescent Vanity Fair	Mrs D. Hodgkinson	Breeder
Ch. Krescent Token	9.4.69	D	Krescent Quando	Krescent Orange Blossom	Mrs D. Hodgkinson	Breeder

Name	D.O.B.	Sex	Sire	Dam	Breeder	Owner
1972						
Ch. Kenlucky Sam	29.8.70	D	Ch. Jokyl Spaceleader	Kenlucky Katrina	Mrs A.L. Jones	Mr & Mrs G. Jackson
Ch. Bengal Mogul	10.8.70	D	Ch. Krescent Token	Ch. Bengal Suliston Merrymaid	Mrs M. Harmsworth	Breeder
Ch. Limebell Rosemary	19.1.70	B	Ch. Jokyl Spaceleader	Bengal Rice	Miss M.K. Young	Breeder
Ch. Tintara Mulberry	29.7.70	B	Siccawei Andros	Ch. Tintara Classical	Mrs P.A. Crome	Breeder
Ch. Jokyl Spic N'Span	24.1.70	D	Ch. Bengal Flamboyant	Ch. Jokyl Elegance	Mr & Mrs G. Jackson	Breeder
Ch. Loudwell Starlight	7.12.70	B	Ch. Jokyl Superior	Loudwell Quest	Mrs J. Campbell	Breeder
Ch. Janella Apollo	15.7.69	D	Ch. Jokyl Spaceleader	Janella Kirtle	Mrs J. Allen-Luckman	Mr G. Hindle
1973						
Ch. Fancy Me of Tanworth	24.9.70	B	Just So of Tanworth	Ch. Fancy Free of Tanworth	Mr & Mrs J. Holland	Miss J. Holland
Ch. Jokyl Cinderella	3.8.70	B	Ch. & Int. Ch. Jokyl Bengal Figaro	Kenlucky Latona	Mrs A.L. Jones	Mr & Mrs G. Jackson
Ch. Ginger Let it Be	10.8.70	B	Italian & Int. Ch. Bengal Bandcola	Bengal Rietbok Ecstacy	Mrs A. Livraghi	Breeder
Ch. Siccawei Ici Moi	26.2.72	B	Ch. Siccawei Kings Ransome	Ch. Siccawei Ruby	Mrs C.M. Halford	Breeder
Ch. Cordwell Derring Do	26.7.73	D	Ch. Optimist of Mynair	Cordwell Bonnisbairn	Mr R. Evans	Mr A. Lodge & Mr A. Jones
Ch. Jokyl Casanova	3.8.70	D	Ch. & Int. Ch. Jokyl Bengal Figaro	Kenlucky Latona	Mrs A.L. Jones	Mr & Mrs G. Jackson
Ch. Lukenia's Trawlerman of Burdale	17.2.72	D	Starcyl Krishna	Tempestuous of Lukenia	Miss A. Irvine	Miss E.M. Jones
Ch. Siccawei Galliard	22.6.70	D	Ch. Bengal Flamboyant	Ch. Siccawei Impudent Miss	Mrs C.M. Halford	Breeder
1974						
Ch. Taltalis Advocate	18.8.71	D	Brulyn Baha Dur	Oakford of Farima	Mr & Mrs S. Takle	Breeder

160

Name	Date	Sex	Sire	Dam	Owner	Breeder
Ch. Loudwell Steadfast	7.12.70	D	Ch. Jokyl Superior	Loudwell Quest	Mrs J. Campbell & Countess Possipucci	Breeder
Ch. Starcyl Krishna	21.9.69	D	Sanbrook Sandpippin	Moira of Kerrydale	Mr & Mrs J. McCrystal	Miss E.M. Jones
Ch. Siccawei Lancastrian	12.12.72	D	Ch. Siccawei Kings Ransome	Siccawei Jess's Postscript	A. & R. Livraghi	Mrs C. Halford
Ch. Wait 'n'See of Jokyl	12.4.73	D	Ch. Jokyl Spic 'n'Span	Kenlucky Latona	Mrs A.L. Jones	Mr & Mrs G. Jackson
Ch. Reptonia Noilly Prat	26.7.72	B	Ch. Siccawei Kings Ransome	Reptonia Framboise	Mr & Mrs R. Back	Breeder
Ch. Bengal Bisquit	8.4.72	B	Ch. Bengal Flamboyant	Bengal Honey Bee	Mrs M. Harmsworth	Breeder
Ch. Tintara Penny Royal	11.4.72	B	Ch. Siccawei Kings Ransome	Ch. Tintara Classical	Mrs P.A. Crome	Mrs P.A. Crome & Mr R. Hill

1975

Name	Date	Sex	Sire	Dam	Owner	Breeder
Ch. Loudwell Flame	20.7.72	B	Loudwell Stranger	Ch. Loudwell Folly	Mrs J. Campbell	Breeder
Ch. Reptonia Peach Brandy	9.1.74	B	Ch. Bengal Flamboyant	Reptonia Kirsch	Mr & Mrs R. Back	Breeder
Ch. Drakehall Delight	5.4.74	B	Ch. Siccawei Galliard	Ch. Siccawei Ruby	Mr E. Sharpe	Mr S. Ahlberg
Ch. Cileeine Penelope	18.1.74	B	Ch. Siccawei Kings Ransome	Siccawei Q E Too	Mrs D. Chapman	Mrs J. Averis
Ch. Jokyl Smart Guy	24.1.74	D	Ch. Bengal Flamboyant	Ch. Jokyl Elegance	Mr & Mrs G. Jackson	Breeder
Ch. Drakehall Derby Day	5.4.74	D	Ch. Siccawei Galliard	Ch. Siccawei Ruby	Mr E. Sharpe	Mr S. Ahlberg

1976

Name	Date	Sex	Sire	Dam	Owner	Breeder
Ch. Derranser Adventuress	19.7.74	B	Ch. Cordwell Derring Do	Mynair Arthurs Girl	Mr A. Jones	Breeder
Ch. Jokyl Rockaline	6.10.73	B	Jokyl Rock 'n'Rush	Moonrose of Jokyl	Mr & Mrs G. Jackson	Breeder
Ch. Jokyl Smartie Pants	29.3.75	B	Ch. Jokyl Smart Guy	Jokyl Dollyrocker	Mr & Mrs G. Jackson	Breeder
Ch. Drakehall Dinah	5.4.74	B	Ch. Siccawei Galliard	Ch. Siccawei Ruby	Mr E. Sharpe	Mr S. Ahlberg
Ch. Tintara Trustee	21.12.74	D	Ch. Siccawei Galliard	Ch. Tintara Penny Royal	Mrs P. Crome	Breeder
Ch. Jokyl Cinerama	9.2.74	D	Ch. Siccawei Galliard	Ch. Jokyl Cinderella	Mr & Mrs G. Jackson	Breeder
Ch. Tanworth Merriment	29.6.75	D	Ch. Jokyl Smart Guy	Tanworth Wy Not Me	Mr & Mrs J. Holland	Breeder

161

Name	D.O.B.	Sex	Sire	Dam	Breeder	Owner
1977						
Ch. Loudwell Venus	19.10.74	B	Loudwell Krisp	Ch. Loudwell Starlight	Mrs J. Campbell	Breeder
Ch. Jenirox Katie Krunch	11.8.75	B	Loudwell Krisp	Jennirox Cora	Mrs H. Dodgson	Breeder
Ch. Bengal Tarquin	16.10.74	D	Ch. Siccawei Lancastrian	Ch. Bengal Bisquit	Mrs M. Harmsworth	Breeder
Ch. Cortella Paper Mate	12.1.75		Innkeeper of Cortella	Jokyl Flirtatious	Mr G. Howells	Breeder
1978						
Ch. Double Dutch of Clare	26.1.76	D	Ch. Drakehall Derby Day	Sueman Cintroid	Messrs Collings & Milner	Messrs Collings & Milner & A. Livraghi
Ch. Turith Brigand	21.5.76	D	Ch. Siccawei Galliard	Prelude of Turith	Mrs B. Blower	Mrs J. Averis
Ch. Bengal Saladin	9.7.76	D	Ch. Bengal Flamboyant	Picturesque of Saredon	Mrs J. Averis	Mrs M. Harmsworth
Ch. Cortella High Society	9.7.76	B	Innkeeper of Cortella	Jokyl Flirtatious	Mr G. Howells	Breeder
Ch. Cloverill Fern	5.3.76	B	Ch. Tintara Trustee	Cloverill Camellia	Mrs M. Hall	Breeder
Ch. Perrancourt Playful	9.2.77	B	American Ch. Turith Adonis	Perrancourt Preview	Mrs D. Hanks	Breeder
Ch. Tintara Upstart	22.5.75	B	Ch. Jokyl Smart Guy	Tintara Persephone	Mrs P. Crome	Breeder
Ch. Be My Guest of Cripsey	5.4.74	B	Ch. Siccawei Galliard	Ch. Siccawei Ruby	Mr E. Sharpe	Mrs P. Havenhand
1979						
Ch. Loudwell Whispers	24.5.77	D	Loudwell Stratford	Loudwell Inspiration	Mrs J. Campbell	Breeder
Ch. Jokyl Happy Guy	24.9.77	D	Ch. Jokyl Smart Guy	Jokyl Baby Talk	Mr & Mrs G. Jackson	Breeder
Ch. Tintara Zealous	7.7.77	D	Ch. Tintara Trustee	Ch. Tintara Upstart	Mrs P. Crome	Breeder
Ch. Hillcross Highboy of Jokyl	25.10.76	B	Ch. Siccawei Galliard	Hillcross Ventora	Mr & Mrs G. Irelan-Hill	Mr & Mrs G. Jackson
1980						
Ch. Bengal Sahib	10.10.78	D	Ch. Bengal Saladin	Carnon Corn Dolly	Mrs A. Nicholls	Mrs M. Harmsworth
Ch. Bengal Carnon Contessa	7.3.78	B	Ch. Bengal Saladin	Carnon Model Maid	Mr A. Hearn	Mrs M. Harmsworth
Ch. Drakehall Debra of Junaken	17.4.77	B	American Ch. Turith Adonis	Ch. Siccawei Ruby	Mr E. Sharpe	Mr K. Ventress

Name	Date	Sex	Sire	Dam	Owner	Breeder
Ch. Jenirox Kizzy	30.5.77	B	New Zealand Ch. Loudwell Krisp	Jenirox Cora	Mrs H. Dodgson	Breeder
Ch. Jokyl Lucy Locket	6.1.78	B	Ch. Siccawei Galliard	Ch. Jokyl Rockaline	Mr & Mrs G. Jackson	Breeder
Ch. Loudwell Vixon	25.8.78	B	New Zealand Ch. Loudwell Krisp	Ch. Loudwell Flame	Mrs J. Campbell	Breeder
Ch. Mynair Never Give in'	19.1.78	D	Mynair Sensation	Mynair I-Liker	Mr A. Lodge	Breeder
1981						
Ch. Saredon Brown Sugar	3.11.78	B	Ch. Turith Brigand	Saredon Strawberry Flair	Mrs J. Averis	Breeder
Ch. Shadli Adorn	9.11.78	B	Wellington of Lyonsdale of Searchlight	Shadli Party Piece	Mr & Mrs A. Favell	Breeder
Ch. Jokyl Fancy Pants	15.9.79	B	Swedish Ch. Jokyl Walkie Talkie	Ch. Jokyl Smartie Pants	Mr & Mrs G. Jackson	Breeder
Ch. Glentops Krackerjack	11.7.78	D	Ch. Turith Brigand	Glentops Eloquence	Mrs B. McCullum	Breeder
Ch. Glentops Ocean Breeze	10.2.80	B	Ch. Glentops Krackerjack	Glentops I'm a Lady	Mrs B. McCullum	Breeder
1982						
Ch. Saredon Super Trouper	16.6.80	D	Saredon Sir Duke	Ch. Saredon Brown Sugar	Mrs J. Averis	Breeder
Ch. Turith Echelon of Saredon	12.7.79	D	Am. Ch. Saredon Military Man	Prelude of Turith	Mrs B. Blower	Mrs J. Averis & Mr D. Scawthorne
Ch. Jokyl Smart Enough	15.9.79	D	Swedish Ch. Jokyl Walkie Talkie	Ch. Jokyl Smartie Pants	Mr & Mrs G. Jackson	Mrs O. Jackson & M. Swash
Ch. Jokyl Hot Gossip of Hillcross	16.9.80	B	Ch. Jokyl Smart Guy	Jokyl Talk of the Town	Mr & Mrs G. Jackson	Mr & Mrs G. Irelan- Hill
Ch. Jokyl Buttons 'n'Bows	23.9.80	B	Ch. Siccawei Galliard	Ch. Jokyl Smartie Pants	Mr & Mrs G. Jackson	Mrs O. Jackson & M. Swash
Ch. Mynair Silver Sunbeam	27.6.80	B	Swedish Ch. Copperstone Hannibal Hayes	Mynair Remember Me	Mr A. Lodge	Mr A. Lodge & Mrs J. Turner
1983						
Ch. Loudwell Nosegay	23.6.80	B	New Zealand & Australian Ch. Loudwell Fife & Drum	Loudwell Bride of Paynor	Mr A. Norcross	Mrs J. Campbell
Ch. Jetstream Summer Moon	29.10.80	B	Saredon Echo of Darinkum	Jetstream Moonlight	Mrs J. Sargeant	Breeder

Name	D.O.B.	Sex	Sire	Dam	Breeder	Owner
Ch. Glentops Ocean Mist	12.2.80	B	Ch. Glentops Krackerjack	Glentops I'm a Lady	Mrs B. McCullum	Breeder
Ch. Jokyl Hot Lips	11.2.82	B	Ch. Siccawei Galliard	Jokyl Hot Pants	Wundpets Ltd (Jackson)	Miss G. Sandahl
Ch. Jokyl Swanky Pants	23.9.80	B	Ch. Siccawei Galliard	Ch. Jokyl Smartie Pants	Wundpets Ltd (Jackson)	Mrs O. Jackson & M. Swash
Ch. Jokyl Gallipants	23.8.81	D	Ch. Siccawei Galliard	Ch. Jokyl Smartie Pants	Wundpets Ltd (Jackson)	Mrs O. Jackson & M. Swash
Ch. Ginger Veronica	22.11.80	B	Ch. Double Dutch of Clare	Drakehall Diadem	Mrs A. Livraghi	Breeder
Ch. The Deerhunter of Saredon	25.7.81	D	Ch. Turith Echelon of Saredon	Saredon Maggie May	J.T.J. Samuel	Mrs J. Averis
1984						
Ch. Glentops Raggitty Ann	27.11.80	B	Ch. Glentops Krackerjack	Danish Ch. Glentops Mischief Maker	Mrs B. McCullum	Breeder
Ch. Perrancourt Pirate	18.10.80	D	Ch. Siccawei Galliard	Ch. Perrancourt Playful	Mrs D. Hanks	Breeder
Ch. Perrancourt Play The Game of Jokyl	17.3.82	B	Ch. Siccawei Galliard	Ch. Perrancourt Playful	Mrs D. Hanks	Mrs O. Jackson and M. Swash
Ch. Jokyl Sunday Best	23.8.81	D	Ch. Siccawei Galliard	Ch. Jokyl Smartie Pants	Wundpets Ltd (Jackson)	Mrs O. Jackson & M. Swash
Ch. Shadli Classy Charmer	15.12.80	B	Ch. Siccawei Galliard	Shadli Party Piece	Mr & Mrs A. Favell	Mr W. Schoneberg
Ch. Cocas Cosmos	24.4.83	D	Cocas Cola	Cocas Topsy Turvey	Mesdames Rendall & Stevens	Breeders
Ch. Karudon Kalypso	19.11.81	B	Jokyl Smart Set	Karudon Kaster Sugar	Mrs R. Millar	Breeder
1985						
Ch. Jimwin Jackpot of Cortella	14.2.83	D	Ch. Jokyl Gallipants	Jimwin Clarinda Clare	Mr M. Jones	Mr G. Howells
Ch. Ginger Xmas Carol	25.12.82	B	Int. Ch. Double Dutch of Clare	Drakehall Diadem	Mrs A. Livraghi	Breeder
Ch. Saredon The Jazzsinger	2.5.83	D	Ch. The Deerhunter of Saredon	Turith Feature of Junaken	Mrs J. Averis	Breeder
Ch. Elbana Prairie	3.10.83	D	Ch. The Deerhunter of Saredon	Mynair Precious Penny	Mr & Mrs G. Anable	Breeder

Name	Date	Sex	Sire	Dam	Owner	Breeder
Ch. Junaken Valldeb	18.3.83	B	Ch. Jokyl Gallipants	Ch. Drakehall Debra of Junaken	Mr K. Ventress	Breeder
Ch. Shadli Phantom	23.12.82	D	Ch. Jokyl Gallipants	Shadli Classy Charmer	Mr & Mrs A. Favell	Breeders

1986

Name	Date	Sex	Sire	Dam	Owner	Breeder
Ch. Stargus Seaking	7.3.84	D	Ch. Perrancourt Pirate	Jokyl Joyful of Stargus	Mrs L. Lee	Breeder
Ch. Beacytan Koh-I-Noor	6.11.84	B	Beacytan Gay Fawkes	Jellibabi of Jomark	Mrs B. Forsman	Breeder
Ch. Beacytan Gay Paree	1.7.83	B	Ch. Jokyl Smart Enough	Beacytan Alison	Mrs B. Forsman	Breeder
Ch. Something Special for Jokyl	15.4.85	B	Ch. Jokyl Gallipants	Sarakel Great Expectations	Mr & Mrs G. Grinham	Mrs O. Jackson & M. Swash
Ch. Jokyl Vivacious	18.8.83	B	Ginger Voila of Stansted	Ch. Jokyl Smartie Pants	Mrs O. Jackson & M. Swash	Miss D. Graham
Ch. Junaken Vanity	26.5.84	B	Ch. Jokyl Gallipants	Ch. Drakehall Debra of Junaken	Mr K. Ventress	Breeder

1987

Name	Date	Sex	Sire	Dam	Owner	Breeder
Ch. Shadli Likely Lad	15.9.85	D	Ginger Voila of Stansted	Shadli Bellona	Mr & Mrs A. Favell	Breeder
Ch. Dendaric Figurehead	27.1.86	B	Ch. Stargus Seaking	Shadli Classy Charisma of Dendaric	Mr & Mrs D. Brown	R. & J. Sawyer
Ch. Jokyl Another Smartie	20.10.85	B	Jokyl Smart Set	Ch. Jokyl Swanky Pants	Mrs O. Jackson & M. Swash	Breeder
Ch. Blackjacks Nostradamus	26.7.84	D	American Ch. Blackjacks Mighty Samson	Chado's Airs 'n' Graces	T. & S. Pesota	Mrs B. Forsman & Miss S. Rosell
Ch. Junaken Valletta	26.5.84	B	Ch. Jokyl Gallipants	Ch. Drakehall Debra of Junaken	Mr K. Ventress	Mrs B. Frost
Ch. Ardessa Emereld Isla	29.7.85	B	Ch. Jokyl Gallipants	Palatinate Solitaire of Junaken	Mrs V. Johnson	W., J. & A. Baker
Ch. Junaken Veejay	31.1.85	B	Ch. Jokyl Gallipants	Ch. Drakehall Debra of Junaken	Mr K. Ventress	Breeder
Ch. Saredon Handyman	15.7.85	D	Saredon Sir Duke	Saredon Heartbreaker	Mrs J. Averis	Breeders
Ch. Junaken Valletta of Beacytan	31.1.85	B	Ch. Jokyl Gallipants	Ch. Drakehall Debra of Junaken	Mr K. Ventress	Mrs B. Forsman

1988

Name	Date	Sex	Sire	Dam	Owner	Breeder
Ch. Shadli Magnum of Robroyd	24.8.86	D	Ch. Jokyl Gallipants	Shadli Bellona	Mr & Mrs A. Favell	Mr & Mrs J. Huxley
Ch. Broen Eyebury Princess	5.11.85	B	Ch. & Am. Ch. Shadli Fantom	Broen Eye Level	Mr R.E. Gould	Breeder

Name	D.O.B.	Sex	Sire	Dam	Breeder	Owner
Ch. Jokyl American Dream	3.9.86	B	Ch. & Am. Ch. Blackjacks Nostradamus	Ch. Jokyl Buttons 'n' Bows	Mrs O. Jackson & M. Swash	Breeders
Ch. Beacytan Serendipity	19.8.86	B	Ch. & Am. Ch. Blackjacks Nostradamus	Beacytan Fantasia	Mrs B. Forsman	Mrs B. Forsman & Mr M. Collings
Ch. Glentops Trick or Treat	26.12.85	D	Ch. Saredon The Jazzsinger	Glentops Yorkshire Rose	Mrs B. McCullum	Breeder
Ch. Saredon September Morn	12.7.86	B	Ch. Saredon The Jazzsinger	Saredon Secret Love	Mrs J. Averis	Breeder
Ch. Junaken Veni Vedi Vici	24.12.86	B	Ch. Saredon The Jazzsinger	Ch. Junaken Valldeb	Mr K. Ventress	Breeder

1989

Name	D.O.B.	Sex	Sire	Dam	Breeder	Owner
Ch. Florac King of Scots at Stargus	16.3.87	D	Ch. Stargus Seaking	Flora Bruichladdich	Mrs F. Whiting	Mrs L. Lee
Ch. Jokyl Hillcross Hotshot	25.10.86	D	Ch. Jokyl Gallipants	Ch. Jokyl Hot Gossip of Hillcross	Mr & Mrs G. Irelan-Hill	Mrs O. Jackson & M. Swash
Ch. Broen Apple of my Eye	21.9.87	B	Shadli Shameless of Broen	Broen Eye Searcher	Mr R. Gould	Breeder
Ch. Jokyl What A Gem	27.3.87	B	Ch. & Am. Ch. Blackjacks Nostradamus	Ch. Jokyl Buttons 'n' Bows	Mrs O. Jackson & M. Swash	Breeder
Ch. Jokyl Liberty Lady	27.3.87	B	Ch. & Am. Ch. Blackjacks Nostradamus	Ch. Jokyl Buttons 'n' Bows	Mrs O. Jackson & M. Swash	Breeder
Ch. Beacytan Vanilla	5.2.87	B	Ch. & Am. Ch. Blackjacks Nostradamus	Beacytan Be A Honey	Mrs B. Forsman	Breeder
Ch. Beacytan Troubadour	8.11.86	D	Ch. & Am. Ch. Blackjacks Nostradamus	Ch. Beacytan Gay Paree	Mrs B. Forsman	Breeder
Ch. Codale Margarite	6.11.86	B	Codale Gotcha	Codale Loxley	Mr G. Dale	Breeder
Ch. McKerros Caledonian Girl	19.12.86	B	Ch. & Am. Ch. Blackjacks Nostradamus	McKerros Aberlady	Mr & Mrs J. Riches	Breeder
Ch. Ballintober Gold of Saredon	10.4.88	D	Ch. Saredon The Jazzsinger	Ch. Junaken Vallotta	Mrs B. Frost	Mrs J. Averis
Ch. Jokyl Something Else	16.12.87	B	Jokyl Treble Chance	Ch. Something Special for Jokyl	Mrs O. Jackson & M. Swash	Breeder

1990

Name	Date	Sex	Sire	Dam	Owner	Breeder
Ch. Dendaric Hot Stuff	4.12.87	B	Dendaric Glen Grant	The Rose of Dendaric	Mr & Mrs D. Brown	Mr & Mrs J. Hicks
Ch. Sunlet Cassandra of Amritsar	12.2.88	B	Junaken Vanguard	Hunslet Cleopatra	M. Barker	Mrs P.R. Storer & Mrs M. Lomax
Ch. Tintara Quickstep	24.9.87	B	Jokyl Smart Set	Tintara Icando	Mrs P.A. Crome	Breeder
Ch. Tondaberi Sweet Chariti	13.1.88	B	Loudwell Battle Oak	Loudwell Silver Slipper at Tondaberi	Mr & Mrs D.M. Warner	Breeder
Ch. Jokyl Lucky Strike	20.2.88	D	Ginger Voila of Stanstead	Ch. Jokyl Another Smartie	Mrs O. Jackson & Mrs M. Swash	Breeder
Ch. Ginger Dancing Song by Jokyl	8.3.88	B	Jokyl Treble Chance	Ch. Ginger Xmas Carol	Mrs A. Livraghi	Miss G. Coxall
Ch. Ginger Daddys Dream	1.10.88	B	Ch. Jokyl Gallipants	Ch. Ginger Xmas Carol	Mrs A. Livraghi	Breeder
Ch. Berrodale Constellation	27.10.88	D	Cocas Comet of Berrodale	Berrodale Clementine	Mrs H. Bush	Breeder
Ch. Beacytan Silver Dollar	19.8.86	D	Am. Eng. & Int. Ch. Blackjacks Nostradamus	Beacytan Fantasia	Mrs B. Forsman	Breeder
Ch. Karudon Kuddle Up	25.4.88	B	Ch. Jokyl Gallipants	Ch. Karudon Kalypso	Mrs R.V. Millar	Breeder

1991

Name	Date	Sex	Sire	Dam	Owner	Breeder
Ch. Nedella Military Salute	11.6.89	D	Ch. Stargus Sea King	Remy's Avenger of Nedella	Mr & Mrs J. Morris	Breeder
Ch. Tintara Royal Salute	11.11.88	D	Ch. Saredon the Jazzsinger	Tintara Icando	Mrs P.A. Crome & Mrs J. Averis	Mrs P.A. Crome
Ch. Beacytan Clairvoyant	26.1.89	B	Berrodale Razzle Dazzle	Beacytan Silver Screen	Mrs B. Forsman	Breeder
Ch. Botarus Galaxy at Jokyl	14.5.89	B	Ch. Jokyl Gallipants	Botarus Copper Gleam	Mr & Mrs B. Mursell	Mr S. Ruxton
Ch. Fast Lady of Cornforth	8.3.89	B	Dendaric Glen Grant	Junaken Vamous	Dr P. Rodgers	R. & N.A. Hamilton
Ch. Jokyl American Express	17.3.90	D	Ch. Jokyl Gallipants	Ch. Jokyl American Dream	Mrs O. Jackson & Mrs M. Swash	Breeder
Ch. Branded Naughty but Nice of Jokyl	9.8.89	B	Ch. Jokyl Gallipants	Midnight Lady of the Manor	Mrs O. Jackson & Mrs M. Swash	Mr D. Brand
Ch. Junaken Vision	6.11.89	B	Ch. Ballintober Gold of Saredon	Ch. Junaken Vee Jay	K Ventress	Breeder
Ch. Saredon Start the Fire	24.5.89	D	Ch. Ballintober Gold of Saredon	Saredon Uptown Girl	J. Averis	J. Averis & D. Scawthorn

Name	D.O.B.	Sex	Sire	Dam	Breeder	Owner
1992						
Ch. Stanstead Shining Star	31.3.90	B	Ch. Jokyl Gallipants	Ch. Jokyl Vivacious	Miss L.D. Graham	Breeder
Ch. Junaken Verdun	1.7.90	B	Ch. Jokyl Gallipants	Junaken Vitality	K. Ventress	Breeder
Ch. Robroyd Emerald	29.10.90	B	Ch. Ballintober Gold of Saredon	Robroyd Crystal	T. & J.E. Huxley	Breeder
Ch. Codale Glint of Gold at Tiggis	3.12.89	B	Ch. Ballintober Gold of Saredon	Ch. Codale Margarite	G. Dale	P.J. & P. Dugdill
Ch. Jokyl G-Force	31.12.89	D	Ch. Jokyl Gallipants	Jokyl Playful Pet	Mrs O. Jackson & Mrs M. Swash	Miss H. Frizell
Ch. Karudon Klose Kontact	25.4.88	D	Ch. Jokyl Gallipants	Ch. Karudon Kalypso	Mrs R.V. Millar	Breeder
Ch. Karudon Karlah	28.10.90	B	Ch. Karudon Klose Kontact	Karudon Katie Maybe	Mrs R.V. Millar	Breeder

Further Reading

Aspinall, J.L. *Ethel, The Airedale Terrier* (1948).

Baker, W.E. *The Airedale Terrier Standard Simplified* (2nd edition 1921).

Bowen, A. *Airedales* (1950).

Bruette, W.A. *The Airedale: a treatise on the History, Breeding and Training* (1916).

Buckley, H. *The Airedale Terrier* (1905).

Edwards, G.B. *The Complete Airedale Terrier* (1962).

Hayes, I.E. *The Airedale Terrier* (1960).

Haynes, W. *The Airedale* (1911).

Hochwalt, A.F. *The Airedale for Work and Show* (1921).

Johns, R. (ed) *Our Friend the Airedale* (1932).

Jowett, F.M. *The Airedale Terrier* (1916).

Miller, W.H. *Airedale Setter and Hound* (1916).

Miller, E. *Airedales as Pets* (1959).

Miller, E. *How to Raise and Train an Airedale* (1960).

Oorang Comments and Oorang Notes. A series of booklets/catalogues issued in the 1920s and 1930s by the kennels of the same name.

Richardson, E.H. This author wrote several extremely interesting books on the training of dogs for war and police work.
  1. *War, Police and Watch Dogs* (1910).
  2. *British War Dogs: their training and psychology* (1920).
  3. *Watch Dogs: their training and management* (1923).
  4. *Forty years with dogs* (1929).
  5. *Fifty years with dogs* (completed by Blanche Richardson) (1950).

Saunders, J. *The Airedale: its history, breeding, showing and general management* (1929).

Saunders, J. *The Modern Airedale: its history, breeding, showing and general management* (1935).

Strebeigh, B. *Pet Airedale Terrier* (1963).

Useful Addresses

The Airedale Terrier Club of
    Scotland
Mrs Barbara Haw
28 Kilmardinny Grove
Bearsden
Glasgow G61 3NY

Midland Counties Airedale
    Terrier Club
Mrs Beryl McCallum
Longford Lodge
Watling Street
Hatherton
Cannock
Staffordshire WS11 1SJ

National Airedale Terrier
    Association
Mrs M. Tarplee
263 Eachelhurst Road
Walmley
Sutton Coldfield
West Midlands

North of England Airedale
    Terrier Club
Mrs B. Bailey
16 Calwell Close
Astley Tyldesley
Greater Manchester
    M29 7FN

Airedale Terrier Club of
    Northern Ireland
Mrs Jean Duke
54 Finaghy Road South
Belfast BT10 0DE

Northumberland & Durham
    Airedale Terrier Club
Mrs P. Jones
11 McDonald Place
Hartlepool
County Durham

South of England Airedale
    Terrier Club
Mrs S.A. Howard
Watchbell House
Hawkes Down Road
Walmer
Deal
Kent

West of England & South
    Wales Airedale Terrier
    Club
Mr R. Laver
`Broadlands'
Wrington Hill
Wrington
Near Bristol
Avon

Yorkshire & Eastern Counties
    Airedale Terrier Club
Mr G. Anable
133 Northlands Road
Winterton
Near Scunthorpe
Humberside DN15 9UL

The Airedale Terrier Club of
    Ireland
Mrs Susan Kealy
76 Crannagh Road
Rathfarnham
Dublin 14

Surrey & Sussex Airedale
    Terrier Club
Miss S. Wilde
Bradus Cottage
Reigate Road
Hookwood
Horley
Surrey RH6 0AU

The Airedale Terrier Training
    Club of Rushmoor
Mrs Margaret Grinham
20 Minley Road
Cove
Farnborough
Hampshire GU14 9RS

Airedale Terrier Rescue
    Services
Mrs Penny Wheble
Birchwood Lodge Kennels &
    Cattery
Woldingham Road
Woldingham
Surrey CR3 7LR

Airedale Terrier Rescue
    Services
Miss S. Wilde
Bradus Cottage
Reigate Road
Hookwood
Horley
Surrey RH6 0AU

USA

Airedale Terrier Club of
    America
Mrs Aletta Moore
Epoch Farm
14181 County Road 40
Carver MN 55315

Index

(Page numbers in italics denote references to illustrations. Ch. denotes Champion.)

British Standard, 23–7, 107, 109
Broadlands Royal Descendant Ch., 126
Broken-haired Terriers, 20
  Scotch, 22
Broen, Apple of my Eye Ch., 148
  Eyebury Princess Ch., 147
brush, bristle, 95
  slicker, 52
Bull Terrier, crosses with, 7
Burdale kennel, 137–40 passim, 149
  Margarite Ch., 140, 141
  Mr Smith Ch., 141

Caesarian section, 45–6
cage, collapsible, 60, 79, 102
Campbell, Mrs Jean, 140
Canine Distemper, 118
Canine Parvovirus, 119
Care, Anna, 129
Carr, T., 20
Challenge Certificates (CCs, tickets), 79
  Reserve, 80
Champion, international, 131
  title, 80
  1946–89, 150–66
Championship Shows, 79–80, 128–9
  judges for, 104–7
character, 17, 24
  and owners, 32
chewers, persistent, 55
children, and Airedales, 66
Cholmondeley Briar Ch., 11, 12, 126
Clarkson's Broadlands Kennel, 126
classes, in shows, 80–2
Clee Courtier Ch., 127
Clonmel kennel, 13, 126
  Bedrock Ch., 126
  Cuddle-Up Ch., 14
  Kitty Ch., 13
  Marvel, 12, 13
  Monarch Ch., 12, 13, 126
  Monarque Ch., 127
coat, 26, 29, 34–5, 36
  stripping, 96–7
Cocas Cosmos Ch., 145
Codale Margarite Ch., 148
colour, 26, 29, 34
  white, in puppies, 46
comb, 95
  fine-toothed, 52
constipation, 122
Copperstone Hannibal Hayes Ch., 144
corneal oedema (blue eye), 120
Covert Dazzle Ch., 127
Crompton Marvel, 12
Crufts, 82
  Best in Show, 83, 143

post-war, 129
cysts, interdigital, 122

Dale, George, 140, 141, 148
Dalziel, Hugh, 8–9
debutant class, 81
Deerhunter of Saredon Ch., 145
Dell, Tuck, 130
Dendaric Figurehead Ch., 147
dew-claws, removal of, 48
diarrhoea, 121–2
diet, 38, 57–8, 93
  and health, 111, 122
  obesity, 64
  sheet, 54
  vegetarian, 58
diseases, 111–24
dog fighting, 8
dolling-up pad, 95, 96
Drakehall, Debra of Junaken, 140
  Dinah Ch., 140, 144, 149
  Dragoon Ch., 149
drinking water, excessive, 114
  supply of, 111
Dumbarton Lass Ch., 13, 14, 126
  Rattler Ch., 13
  Sceptre Ch., 13
  Sunflower Ch., 13

ears, 24, 27, 34, 124
  breeding, 40
  carriage, 55
ectoparasites, 116–18
eczema, 122
Edwards, A.J. 'Towyn', 127
Edwards, J.M., 20
Elbana Prairie Ch., 146
elbows, 29
Elder G.H., and Tone kennel, 13, 126
endoparasites, 114–16
Exemption Shows, 78
exercise, 73, 93, 111, 112, 122
  routine, 62
eyebrows, trimming, 100
eyes, 24, 28, 34, 36, 124

faults, 27, 30
feeding, bitch, 47
  regurgitation, by bitch, 54
  routine, 62
  puppies, 41, 50, 53
    bottle, 46
    colostrum, 46
    cost of, 40–1, 53
    meals, number of, 54–5
    supplementary, 49
  weaning, 50–1

00182 4575